the tale of
TIBET

the tale of TIBET

Anita Kainthla

Foreword by

His Holiness the Dalai Lama

Viva Books

New Delhi | Mumbai | Chennai | Kolkata | Bengaluru | Hyderabad | Kochi | Guwahati

Publisher's note

Every possible effort has been made to ensure that the information contained in this book is accurate at the time of going to press, and the publisher and author cannot accept responsibility for any errors or omissions, however caused. No responsibility for loss or damage occasioned to any person acting, or refraining from action, as a result of the material in this publication can be accepted by the editor, the publisher or the author.

Every effort has been made to trace the owners of copyright material used in this book. The author and the publisher will be grateful for any omission brought to their notice for acknowledgement in the future editions of the book.

First Published 2011

Viva Books Private Limited

- 4737/23, Ansari Road, Daryaganj, New Delhi 110 002
  Tel. 42242200, 23258325, 23283121, Email: vivadelhi@vivagroupindia.net
- 76, Service Industries, Shirvane, Sector 1, Nerul, Navi Mumbai 400 706
  Tel. 27721273, 27721274, Email: vivamumbai@vivagroupindia.net
- Jamals Fazal Chambers, 26 Greams Road, Chennai 600 006
  Tel. 28294241, 28290304, Email: vivachennai@vivagroupindia.net
- B-103, Jindal Towers, 21/1A/3 Darga Road, Kolkata 700 017
  Tel. 22816713, Email: vivakolkata@vivagroupindia.net
- 7, GF, Sovereign Park Aptts., 56-58, K. R. Road, Basavanagudi, Bengaluru 560 004
  Tel. 26607409, Email: vivabangalore@vivagroupindia.net
- 101-102, Moghal Marc Apartments, 3-4-637 to 641, Narayanguda, Hyderabad 500 029
  Tel. 27564481, Email: vivahyderabad@vivagroupindia.net
- First Floor, Beevi Towers, SRM Road, Kaloor, Kochi 682 018
  Tel. 0484-2403055, 2403056, Email: vivakochi@vivagroupindia.net
- 232, GNB Road, Beside UCO Bank, Silpukhuri, Guwahati 781 003
  Tel. 0361-2666386, Email: vivaguwahati@vivagroupindia.net

www.vivagroupindia.com

ISBN: 978-81-309-1715-3

Published by Vinod Vasishtha for Viva Books Private Limited, 4737/23 Ansari Road, Daryaganj, New Delhi 110 002.

Printed & bound by Sanat Printers, Kundli 131 028.

S0600/X0000

Contents

The author with the Prime Minister of the Tibetan Government in Exile

Foreword

Today, at a time when the Tibetan people are facing many difficulties, many people who have some understanding of the situation in Tibet may not be aware of the country's history. This book makes a useful contribution to filling that gap. The author tells the tale of Tibet, recounting first the myths of the origin of the land and its people and then what historical documents record. She explains how Tibet was once a major military power in Central Asia, exerting its influence throughout Central Asia and beyond into neighbouring territories. Because King Songtsen Gampo was powerful, his neighbours China and Nepal sought to create friendly relations with him through marriage. The two princesses who were sent to be his wives brought with them statues of the Buddha which were housed in what became the first temples in Tibet. So began Tibet's interest in Buddhism.

On the one hand, Buddhism, with its peaceful outlook and emphasis on non-violence, diminished Tibetan military inclinations, but on the other it became the source of a completely different kind of influence – an influence based on knowledge. For more than a thousand years Tibetans have been custodians of the full range of the Buddha's teachings. These have been analysed, refined and most important of all put into practice, becoming the mainstay of Tibetan culture. Living experience of Buddhist meditation has given practitioners a profound knowledge of the workings and nature of the mind, an inner science to complement the perhaps better known science of the outer world.

Readers can find out here not only how Tibet was shaped by Buddhist traditions, but also how those traditions came about and originally flourished in India itself. Here is evidence of the indisputably strong ties that have long existed between Tibetans and Indians, and which I pray will continue to thrive long into the future.

Dalai Lama

2 August 2010

1
The Beginning

IN THE PAST FEW DECADES the tale of Tibet has aroused intrigue the world over, in general, and the West in particular. As recounted in traditional Tibetan sources, the story begins in the distant past when the land of Tibet had recently risen above water. This aspect of the story corresponds to recently found scientific information on the area's geographical history. In the distant past much of what is now the Tibetan plateau was under water, but approximately 40 million years ago the Indian landmass collided with Asia and it began to slide underneath the Asian landmass, eventually lifting up the land that had been under water. One of its results was the formation of the Himalayas, and a huge high altitude plateau that came to form the country of Tibet.

For many centuries Tibet remained virtually unknown to the rest of the world (and vice versa) being entombed by the impenetrable Himalayas. Only in the middle of the last century, the great dramatic escape of the spiritual and political heir of Tibet, the fourteenth Dalai Lama, from the clutches of the Chinese communist regime, set the world's curious gaze upon it. A sensation broke loose over the world in the wake of this audacious escape. As an outcome Tibet emerged from the obscurity of its formidable mountains only to be submerged beneath the world's curious conjectures regarding its history, geography, politics—its story at large.

Tibet's tale is set in the highest and the largest plateau on the earth, bordered on three sides by mountain ranges, towering over the central part of Asia. Little wonder then, for the country to be nicked 'Roof of the World'. This 'Roof' is walled by the great Himalayan Mountains to the south, which extends for 1,500mi., and Altyn Tagh and Gankar Chogley Namgyal Mountains in the north. While its western portion merges with the Karakoram Mountains, the eastern one gracefully slopes downward with the Minyak Gangkar and Khawa Karpo Mountains. It soars above the sea level at a height of 3,650m., with most of its peaks looming beyond 8,000m. The tallest, Mount Everest (Mt. Chomo Lungma, for Tibetans), is among the proudest possessions of the country's mountain ranges.

Tibet is bordered by mountains on three sides, with a break only in the east. Much of the area encompassed by Tibet's border mountains which lie at 16,000ft. and above make it inhospitable to humans as such climatic conditions are unable to support vegetation. Tibet is a vast land with sparse population spread over high plateaus and three-sevenths of Tibet is a virtually uninhabited wilderness of mountain spurs and ranges, interspersed with black barren plains and numerous pools and lakes of brackish water. Ensconced in the heart of Asia, with India, Nepal, Bhutan, Myanmar lying to its north and China spread along its western and southern portion, Tibet's history and geography, like no other country's in the world, inevitably invokes both wonder and curiosity.

In this cold, dry and inaccessible terra incognita of Tibet, the Mongoloid peoples are spread over three major geographical sub-divisions of the country—Amdo (Domed), Dotod (Kham) and U-Tsang.

Rife among the Tibetan population are a couple of interesting mythological episodes which attempt an explanation of their origins. According to one Tibetan legend, the Tibet of eons ago was a country of ravines, mountaintops and torrents, varied by huge lakes. Then one day Buddha visited this land in person and discovered that the inhabitants here were monkeys. Astonished, he questioned the monkeys as to why they were not men and good Buddhists. The monkeys, in answer, told him that with the country's existing geographical state, there was absolutely no opportunity for the development of their bodies, let alone their religious impulses. And then the Buddha said to them, 'if you will promise to become men and good Buddhists, I will give you a good and fertile land to live on.' And having said so, the Buddha, in his immense compassion, drained off the waters from the land by an underground channel through the Himalayas into the Ganges near Gaya, in the Indian state of Bihar. This is now known as the plain of Gyantse. The Tibetans in turn kept their promise by becoming both civilized men and devoted Buddhists.

Through a more popular parable, the Tibetans claim that their first parent was a monkey that crossed the Himalayas and married a she-devil of the mountains. A young progeny of the apes ate some magical grains given to them by the compassionate spirit of the mountains—who afterwards became the Grand Lama; the results were amazing. Their tails and hair grew shorter and shorter till they finally disappeared.

Gradually they discovered speech and finally became men. The occurrence of ancestors as monkeys in both the legends makes one wonder whether these legends have drawn inspiration from Darwin's theory of evolution. But whatever the basis of these spicy mythical bits, they yet remain only in the form of legends hard to consume and digest.

A popular origin myth of early Tibet contends that its first king came from India. According to one account, he was born with unusual physical attributes, including long blue eyebrows and webbed fingers. Ostracised by his people, he wandered north, eventually coming to Tibet. In another version, he was a refugee of an Indian war, which took place between the Kurus and Pandavas, and is recounted in the epic of the Mahabharata. Disguising himself as a woman, he crossed the Himalayas and met some people living in caves on the high plateau. People he met asked him where was he coming from. Unable to understand their question, he pointed towards the sky. Those who saw this decided that he had descended from the heavens and proposed to make him king, since at that time they had no ruler. They placed him on their shoulders and carried him to their village; and so he came to be called Nyatri Tsenpo, meaning 'Neck-enthroned king'. According to legend he built Tibet's largest house and began introducing Indian civilization. He is considered to be the first of the kings of the earliest ruling dynasty of Tibet, which has its capital near the Tsangpo river in the Yarlung Valley, about 55mi. southeast of Lhasa.

The Chinese sources, however, link the origin of the Tibetan people to the nomadic, non-Chinese Chiang tribes, who herded sheep and cattle from the east of Central Asia up to the farthest north western borders of China, much before the Christian era. They gathered this extensive nature of Tibetan farming with its ever present element of animal husbandry, from the readiness of the Tibetans to travel long distances, their seemingly inborn ability to handle and look after horses, yaks and other animal, their delight in open air and open spaces and their sturdy individualism. The most important part of this legacy was the presence of a large number of nomads, depending entirely on their flock of sheep and goats and herds of yak. They lived a nomadic life, camping in tents and were divided into constantly warring clans. Chinese considered them as an assemblage of ferocious, barbarous tribes. Each of these clans presumably consisted of a chief with his family and hereditary retainers and bondsmen. When they settled down, the chief's family became a kind of aristocracy. A world of rival chiefs then came into existence, with their fortified strongholds in the valleys of the central and eastern tributaries of the Tsangpo. To the north of these were areas inhabited by nomadic people who often displaced tribes that had already settled permanently. This went on till the sixth century AD. Central Tibet then took the offensive, and the infiltrations from the North East ceased, except for certain rare alliances. During these developments some local chiefs accepted the powerful chief who ruled Yarlung valley as their overlord, backing him as a king strong enough to force his neighbours to take notice of his pre-eminence.

Like any other ancient country, even in the case of Tibet, no one story of its origins can provide convincing links to bridge the breaks between myth and history. Much of Tibet's recorded history begins after the advent of Buddhism into the country, as Buddhism brought literacy and culture into Tibet.

Pre-Buddhist history is sketchy and patchy and does not offer much.

The pioneers of Tibetan education had their own education in India, presumably at some Buddhist Vihara. The Tibetan script was modeled on the structure of the Indian script. Knowledge of Buddhism was the epitome of Tibetan learning and up till the fourteenth century the translation of an Indian text by an Indian Pandita (scholar) was the most preferred academic endeavour for Tibetan scholars. Therefore earliest of Tibetan historians, do not have any sense of history independent of Buddhist faith and they give no importance to political or economic events. Thus Tibetan history as told by historians is religious and dogmatic. The earliest of the Tibetan historians are historians of Buddhism; politics for them is of an incidental importance. Quoting Petech, 'in "In the Lamaist Chronicles", the history of Tibetan monarchy is nothing but a pretext for edifying tales, or, at the most, the framework in which the life and work of the great apostles of Buddhism are bound together. A little more than the skeleton of the history of the dynasty and almost nothing of the nation has been saved from the general shipwreck.' But religion did play an overtly important role in the making of Tibetan history and even real political struggles were often carried on under religious pretexts.

According to early writings, the pre-Buddhist period up to sixth century in Tibet was that of a religion called Bon; Bon spread over a vast area—from Turkey to Siberia—depended greatly on the exercise of supernatural powers and was believed to be founded by Shenrad Miwo of Shang Shung, in western Tibet. Interestingly some followers of Bon religion maintain that he was a contemporary of Buddha, while others more boldly consider him the incarnation of Buddha. However, traditionally Bon is characterized negatively and viewed as a perversion of Buddhism. It is also often compared to Shamanism. Entombed by the impregnable Himalayas, cut off from even its immediate neighbours and left to the mercy of the formidable clements of nature, the Tibetans began believing that the hazards of everyday life could be prevented by worshipping the mighty nature. Spirits—good and evil—were created, conjured and in time were converted into gods who were propitiated to secure help. The specialist priests, called Shamans, attempted to control nature through their knowledge of propitiating the spirits.

The ancient caravan routes that long linked the literate cultures of Asia avoided the formidable mountains of Tibet and the Tibetan people likewise. For this reason, although Tibet was surrounded by literate societies for centuries, yet it remained the follower of an animistic religion like Bon. It is essentially a shamanist and devil charming necromantic culture and is similar to Taoism of China. Sacrifices of animals and even human beings were openly carried out and this constituted an essential prerequisite for worship.

On the whole Bon had a highly complicated ritualistic system, whereas its religious structure was modest and simple. Official Chinese histories of the fifth and sixth centuries, provide descriptions of gory religious rites including: human sacrifices. 'The officers (Tibetan) are assembled once every year for the lesser oath of fealty. They sacrifice sheep, dogs and monkeys, first breaking their legs and then killing them afterwards, exposing the intestines and cutting them into pieces.' After summoning the sorcerers, they call on the gods of heaven and earth, of the mountains and rivers, of the sun, moon, stars and planets, saying: 'should your hearts become changed, and your thoughts disloyal, the gods will be clearly angry and make you like these sheep and dogs'. Every third year there is a grand ceremony, during which all are assembled in the night on a raised alter, on which are spread savoury meats. The victims sacrificed are men, horses, oxen and asses, and prayers like these are offered: 'do you all, with one heart and united strength, cherish our native country. The god of heaven and the spirit of the earth will both know your thoughts and if you break this oath, they will cause your bodies to be cut into pieces like these victims'.

Bon is forbidden by the lamaist hierarchy who rule in central and western Tibet, but is openly professed in the predominant parts of eastern and south-eastern Tibet—the most populous part of the country.

The entry of Buddhism into Tibet, in its early stages, was cautious and conciliatory. Its adherents obtained permission and protection of the King, Srong Brtsan Sgam Po to practice this religion. Royal patronage was forthcoming for Buddhism as it had the political potential of solving disputes and rivalries between different groups of nobles and ministers. Buddhism also served as a humanizing force for the otherwise rough and warlike people. According to contemporary evidence, contentment and compromise was the popular world view that governed its practitioners and it only sought for peaceful co-existence with Bon.

The hostility or rivalry today between the Buddhists and the Bon po (po – stands for plural of Bon) stems from their ignorance of the extent of the amalgamation that both have undergone. For instance both use the term 'Sangs rgyas' (amply purified) for a perfected sage or a Buddha. By accepting many Buddhist forms, rites and observances and by allowing many Bon practices to be incorporated into Tibetan Buddhism, the Bon po have achieved the status of 'nang pa' or insiders.

Even though there exist fundamental differences between the Buddhists and the Bon po, amalgamations of doctrines and religious practices have been successful in distinct realms. All Buddhists acknowledge the Indian origin of their doctrine and continue to hold the Buddha, Sakyamuni, in deepest reverence. The Bon po on the other hand claim that Buddhist teachings came from a country called sTag gZigs (Iran in a vague sense) and that the original Buddha was gShen rab mi bo, not Sakyamuni. Nonetheless the Bon po, like the Buddhists, perform rituals as prescribed by their religion with the pious intention of eventually becoming 'awakened' and with unquestioning faith on their Buddha; so in this sense they may be considered as profoundly Buddhists. Certainly their monks consider themselves 'sons of the Buddha' – as per their own religion.

Bon, though supported by aristocrats and nobles had to struggle for survival in the face of the challenge from Buddhism. Conflicts and even persecution of the Bon po by the Royal guards took place. Hence some adherents of Bon were forced to become Buddhists; many others were expelled or went into exile after being humiliated. The intelligent among the Bon po recognized the superiority of spiritual and cultural aspects of Buddhism and realized the importance of a single philosophical or religious doctrinal structure. They adopted modes of operation through which they were able to enrich their discipline without jeopardizing their original identity. For this purpose, Bon priests were invited from Shang Shung, an independent country at that time, to assist in the translation of Bon texts. A reconciliation or compromise with Buddhism was made by the Bon po to escape social discrimination and persecution.

Indian Buddhism during the eighth century provided Tibetan Buddhism with a host of gods of varying characteristics. The Bon po found that they could not use the same names for their gods as the Buddhists used. Doing so would mean a loss of identity. They therefore conceived a hierarchy of gods corresponding to the Buddhist ones, but only with a few names. They absorbed all that they possibly could from Buddhist theory and practice. They developed their doctrines on the pattern of the Buddhist theology but adapted them to Bon terminology. The Buddhists too adopted all the beliefs that the local population considered important. Thus many indigenous Tibetan divinities made their way into the Tibetan Buddhist pantheon. King Khri srong, however, showed a propensity towards Buddhism and along with his ministers swore an oath to uphold the Buddhist law. He appointed Buddhist monks as ministers giving them higher ranks than their Bon counterparts. But one of the king's wives was a Bon practitioner, compelling the king to respect the interests of the Bonists, even while opposing the Tibetan nobles. However, in due course of time the king in a burst of fortitude acquired strength openly to express his inclination towards Buddhism. A religious struggle followed, and Bon po was persecuted. The Bon po were forced to accept the new religion. Those who did not comply were banished. The fleeing Bon po hid their books under rocks, which were recovered later in the eleventh century AD.

In ancient times Bon had no monastic system like Buddhism. All ceremonies were mostly performed out in the open. Bon religious centres were confined to the houses or tents of the priests. With the ushering in of Buddhism, however, the Bon po in its likeness began the development of an organized religious life and by the fourteenth century they had organized their teachings in terms of the nine ways. These followed from an orderly arrangement of the various religious practices, both pre-Buddhist and Buddhist.

Bon po today has a monastic tradition in which there is a system of dialectical debate. Its aim is to lend the practitioner an understanding of the illusory nature of the phenomenal world, the impermanence of one's state of being, which is subject to the laws of cause and effect. They believe that release from cyclic existence, resulting from cause and effect must be sought in order to escape from suffering and to gain enlightenment. Despite this monastic tradition, Bon is not a religion in the proper sense as it does not satisfy the prescribed prerequisites of a religion – it has no monasteries, no temples, no brotherhood of priests and there is no central doctrine to bind people together in a common belief system. Before the advent of Buddhism, the early Tibetans had no such strength; their only rescue was to submit to the forces of nature. Their religious beliefs were simple practices that were designed to secure help and to avert harm. But by the time Buddhism entered Tibet Bon already had gathered some foreign elements. For example, the Indian theories of karma and rebirth held their fascination and these were assimilated into Bon. Later Bon also included Buddhist ideas into its belief and thus became a blend of several elements—belief in the divine nature of kings, worship of associated gods, and prevalence of Iranian ideas on the formation of the world. Though earlier Bon existed peacefully along with Buddhism, constant friction between the two was inevitable, as the latter gradually gripped the lives of the people of Tibet.

2

Advent and Advancement of Buddhism

BUDDHISM MOULDED the thought, idea and literature of entire Asia, as early as third century BC, but it was not before the eight century AD that the military expansion of its ancient monarchy brought the Tibetans in contact with the advanced civilizations of China and India and Buddhism penetrated the isolated 'Land of Snows'. However, tradition affirms that by the fourth century AD Buddhist texts were already present in Tibet. In accordance with this tradition, a chest containing Buddhist sacred books and a golden 'chaitya' fell from the sky on the roof of the Tibetan King To-to-ri's palace. The 60-year-old king worshipped these heavenly gifts and as a result lived for 120 years. It was revealed to him in a dream that his fourth successor would know the meaning of the sacred writings. But in actual fact, the king was illiterate and hence incapable of understanding the purport of the texts, which were brought by a Pandit Lo-sem-tso and a translator Li-te-se, from India. It was not until the rule of the illustrious King Sron-btsan-gampo that efforts were made to translate those texts.

Just as Indian history begins to be recorded in writing from the days of the great Buddhist Emperor Ashoka, Tibetan history too was written during the reign of Tibet's most gifted ruler – Sron-btsan-gampo, who first gave the idea of reducing spoken Tibetan into a system of alphabetic writing to facilitate the advent of Buddhism from India into Tibet. Although Buddhism had come to Tibet under such favourable auspices, it did not take root in a foreign soil as quickly and as easily as Gampo might have wished. It had to wage an incessant and arduous struggle for over three centuries against the indigenous Bon beliefs. It had to remove old superstitions, make compromises and adapt its doctrines to the strange customs and traditions which having come down through the ages were deeply rooted in Tibetan psyche. It had to suffer setbacks and banishment from the very beginning, but with the single-minded persistence of several progressive rulers, it finally was able to establish itself as the national religion of the 'Roof of the World'.

Tibet, before the introduction of Buddhism was the greatest military power in Asia. In the early part of the sixth century the Tibetan army conquered and annexed large areas of Central Asia that lay between Tibet and China and were inhabited by nomadic and semi-nomadic tribes of Turkic and Tibetan stock. In 635 BC Tibet attacked China, and in successive campaigns managed to wrest control over large areas that had been under Chinese control. These included the four main Chinese strongholds in Chinese Turkestan. As a result, China lost its lines of communication with the west. In light of its later conversion to Buddhism, it is interesting that Tibet first came into contact with Buddhism as an invading force that ransacked Buddhist institutions in Central Asia and put many monks to death during its military incursions. Surviving records from Tibet's Central Asian neighbours speak of the Tibetan soldiers as the dreaded 'Red Faces', who painted their faces with red ochre and savagely attacked Buddhist institutions, destroying all in their path.

In the third century BC Ashoka made Buddhism the predominant religion of India, where it continued so for the next five hundred years. From the second century of the Christian era, Hinduism flourished at the expense of Buddhism. But the invaders, who came to India from the north-west, favoured the Buddhists over the Hindus, as caste restrictions in Hinduism prevented them from freely mixing with everyone. King Ashoka's contribution in propagation of Buddhism is noteworthy. He dispatched missionaries to various countries for the advancement of religion.

Among the founders of world religions, Buddha was the only teacher who did not claim authority in any form. He attributed all his realization, attainments and achievements to human endeavour and human intelligence. His philosophy is entirely based on observation and reasoning. This philosophy of simple logic, advocating virtues of non-violence and compassion struck a chord in the hearts of the spirited Tibetans. The pacific teachings of Buddhism resulted in the subsequent peacefulness of a war ravaged Tibet. Noted historian Charles Bell has observed that, 'As Buddhism increased preaching peace and forbidding the taking of life, the warlike propensities of the Tibetan tribals diminished. Internecine contests continued, for in the large monasteries itself, there have been many monks ready for local fights and forays. It is in the blood. But from now onwards, external aggression died away. And when with its changed attitude Tibet went to war, it had often to suffer defeat.

Thus more and more it fell under domination of Mongols and other non-Buddhist invaders from the north. However, the Mongols too later converted to Buddhism and their power also declined and Tibet sometimes actually sometimes nominally fell under the sway of China.'

The unification of the country under a single religion was another bane of Buddhism to Tibet. In times to come, as Buddhism was to take deeper and stronger root in the country, Tibet would owe gratitude to it for another important acquisition—the art of reading and writing. However, Buddhism's great journey from India to Tibet was an arduous one, intermittently threatened with curtailment at the hands of some anti-Buddhist propagandists and kings. But fortunately for Tibet and her people in the seventh century BC the great King Sron-btsan-gampo ascended the throne in his thirteenth year, and with unflagging fortitude he not only fought all opposition to Buddhism but also strove to establish it as a national religion. Due to the efforts of this great king, Tibet entered into her classical age in the seventh century.

As with the histories of other ancient countries, the history of Tibet is also part mythology, part mystery. The myth proclaims that a descendent of an Indian King Rupati exiled from the great Magadhan Empire of India, renamed Nyatri Tsenpo was elected the ruler of Yarlung in 127 BC. He is credited with establishing the Purgyal dynasty, and constructing the first fort in Tibet-Yumbu Lagar. The Purgyal dynasty enjoyed a successful reign over Yarlung uptill its eighth king—Drigum Sampo. Unfortunately during Tsenpo's rule, the orthodox Bon religionists rose in revolt and Tsenpo not only lost power for more than a decade but also saw the banishment of his two sons to Kongpo. However, later his younger son—Jatri Tsumpo, regained power and constructed his father's tomb – the first tomb of a king in Yarlung. Jatri's rule was popular as during his reign iron and copper were discovered and metal based technology was developed. He also dug irrigational canals, built bridges and erected a palace called, 'Chingwasr Taktse' at Chongyas. Thus Jatri was responsible for consolidating the rule of the Purgyal dynasty, begun by an exiled Indian ruler.

Eighteen rulers succeeded Jatri. It was during the reign of the twenty-eighth king To-to-ri, of this mighty dynasty, that the books of scripture came to him (probably as a gift on his sixtieth birthday); these Sanskrit books though amply revered by the illiterate and the aging king, went without being translated for a long time. Three generations later, a son was born to the thirty-second ruler of the Purgyal dynasty—Namri Songtsen in AD 617. The young prince named Tri Songtsen was none other than Sron-btsan-gampo in later years. Gampo was really one of the greatest kings of Tibet under whose leadership the Tibetans moved from barbarism to civilization. Under him the political unification of Tibet became fully consolidated. He ascended the throne at thirteen years of age and brought under his control all the petty chieftens. He introduced legal codes into Tibet and established punishments for murder, robbery and adultery. From China he brought silkworms, mulberry trees, barley beer, paper, ink and calendar. He first married the Nepalese princess Bhrikuti, the daughter of King Amsuvarman and later he also took another wife—a Chinese princess. But his marriage to the Chinese princess was not a result of peaceful negotiation. In AD 634, the Emperor of China exchanged presents with the Tibetan king and made a treaty of friendship.

The Tibetans requested for the hand of the Chinese imperial princess for the king that was refused and Tibet invaded China with an army of 200,000 men and fought for eight years. In AD 641, the Chinese empire was finally forced to agree, and married off the princess to Gampo. The princess was a devout Buddhist, due to which the king not only favoured Buddhism over Bon but also aided and strengthened his resolve in the spread of Buddhism in Tibet.

Gampo sent to India his learned minister Thon-mi-Sambhota, along with sixteen other people. Unfortunately due to an arduous journey between the two nations and the extreme weather conditions all of the seventeen members except Sambhota perished. Sambhota, the father of Tibetan literature, returned to Tibet after several years with his knowledge of the Gupta Brahmi script consisting of 34 letters. Before seventh century AD there was no form of writing in Tibet, hence Buddhist texts were memorized and transmitted orally. Gampo's period is considered as the 'Golden Age' in the history of Tibet due to political, cultural and economic progress in the country.

But Chinese sources, says Waddell, 'Show him actively engaged throughout his life in the pursuit of bloody wars with neighbouring states'. He was not the saintly person the grateful lamas pictured him to be, for he is seen in Chinese history to be more on the battlefield than in the temple. And he certainly did very little to promote Buddhism besides translating a few texts into Tibetan and building a few temples to shrine the images received by him in dower and others which he constructed. He built no monasteries either.

However there is evidence that Buddhism was introduced into Tibet during the reign of Sron-btsan-gampo; for there are temples of that period like Jo Khang (which has been greatly enlarged and transformed over the centuries), dBu ru ka tshal (east of Lhasa), Khra 'bong (in the Yarlung Valley) and Rampoche (in Lhasa itself). There is no evidence, however, that the king himself adopted Buddhism. Nor is there any mention of Buddhism in contemporary literary sources. On the other hand the king seems to have been loyal to his ancestral religion, Bon.

In introducing Buddhism into Tibet the king appears to have had political motives rather than religious once. Through his conquest of a number of Central Asian states and his contacts with India (including Kashmir), China and Nepal, which were all flourishing centres of Buddhist culture, he became acquainted with certain elements of that culture such as its universalistic perspective, and felt that Tibet would imbibe those elements without inviting any foreign political influence. Secondly he wanted to introduce the art of writing into Tibet. He finally chose Buddhism from India and many other aspects of Indian culture. One cannot, however, tell that Buddhism was really present in Tibet during the rule of Sron-btsan-gampo. It appears that the king made use of the new religion for the advancement of culture. It was only during the following century (in the rule of King Khri srong Ide brtsan) that one finds mention of Buddhism in official documents. In any case it is clear that Buddhism was established in Tibet under royal patronage and it served and increased royal power.

The eighth century was witness to the emergence of another powerful king, Khri srong Ide brtsan, second only to Gampo in greatness. Khri srong like his forefathers was an ardent Buddhist. During his illustrious reign he worked for Buddhist teachings throughout the country. A couple of brtsan's own ministers were Bon religionists who did not look too kindly upon Buddhism, so much so that they even got a ban imposed on it when he was a minor. Dismissing these ministers, he later requested, Savant Shantirakshita, an Indian, to come to Tibet to teach Buddhism. But the scholar saw that the situation for preaching Buddhism was not very conducive at that time. It stirred up a great resistance, supposedly because the new codes of moral conduct preached by them were directly opposed to the age-old practices of the Bon religion. His teachings, says the famous historian Bu-ston, 'brought the malignant deities of Tibet into a fury. Phan-than was carried away by a flood, lightening struck dMar-po-ri, and diseases befalling men and cattle broke out. The Tibetan subjects declared that this was a consequence of the propagation of a false doctrine, and the acharya (teacher) was sent back to Nepal'. Shantirakshita, thus, had to leave Tibet. But the king, on his advice, agreed to invite the great Tantrika and Vajrayana Buddhist teacher Padmasambhava, to tackle the Tibetan devils and demi-gods. Padmasambhava, with his magical powers, subdued all local devils and demi-gods. This created conditions for Shantirakshita to go back to Tibet and with the help of the King Khri srong, built the monastery of bsam-yas, on the lines of the one at Odantapuri in Bihar in India. This monastery is popularly called Samye monastery. Shantirakshita also trained seven meritorious Tibetans to become the first Tibetan Buddhist monks. This training proved successful and came to be adopted as a model for training monks thereafter. He is also credited with the establishment of the study of Sanskrit language at the Samye monastery.

Guru Padmasambhava, also known as the 'Lotus Born' or 'Rin po che' or 'Precious Guru' or 'Sacred Buddha' is revered by all sects of Tibetan Buddhism. He occupies a place of prominence, sometimes along with the Buddha. He is worshipped in all important monasteries of Tibet. During the later part of the eighth century Padmasambhava was recommended to the king of Tibet by some of India's most famous scholars as one who was the greatest masters of the occult sciences known at that time. Padmasambhava accepted the invitation and went to Tibet in AD 747 to quell the general resistance to Buddhism in Tibet. He is believed to have pacified all inimical forces, only sparing their lives after they swore a solemn oath to preserve the doctrine of the Buddha. This episode is preserved in an elaborate legend, possibly to assimilate or accommodate the local deities of Buddhism. The Tibetans, who were steeped in superstition, welcomed the guru in fervent belief that he had brought the deliverance from their torments. Padmasambhava is also considered to be the founder of Lamaism. 'Lama' is a Tibetan word, meaning a man of superior status. Earlier its use was restricted only to the head of a monastery but the title is now given to almost all Tibetan monks and priests, out of respect. The guru gave a form of Buddhism which proved attractive to the people and it soon became popular. Its doctrine of karma or of ethical retribution, appealed to the fatalism which the Tibetans shared with most eastern races. He attempted to discover a religion of his own in Tibet and even succeeded to some extent, but it had to prematurely depart in the face of opposition from Bon priests and politically powerful ministers.

King Khri srong was possibly the greatest patrons of Buddhism. He brought two of the most learned gurus of India to Tibet. Khri srong was succeeded by his son Muni Tsenpo, whose rule came to an abrupt and awful end because of the treachery of his own mother, as she was jealous of her son's stepmother. His mother poisoned him since he protected his stepmother from his own mother's attack. He was succeeded by his brother Tri Songtsen in AD 804 and Tri Songtsen's successor was one of his younger sons—Ral pa chen, who was enthroned in AD 815.

Ral pa chen was a king, in the league of his great forefathers—Gampo and Khri Srong. In addition to strengthening the translation work of various treatises from Sanskrit to Tibetan, he is also famous for his contribution to the process of modernizing and standardizing the Tibetan language. He encouraged Buddhist literature and a number of texts were then translated. New translations were made only from the originals from India. A list of books was drawn, which were deemed to contain the authentic teaching. The king's personal relations with the Buddhist monks were almost legendry. He left nothing undone to further the interests of the Buddhist clergy and helped to strengthen their position. Real power in the state passed gradually into the hands of the Buddhists. As a fanatic patron of Buddhism, he appointed a Buddhist monk as his chief minister. He also ordered that seven households should be responsible for the maintenance of one Buddhist monk. As a natural consequence of the king's ardent devotion to Buddhism, the ire of the anti-Buddhist faction climaxed. In time this anti-Buddhist faction murdered the Buddhist minister and then in AD 838, assassinated the king. After the assassination of Ral pa chen, followed a period of political disorder. He was succeeded by his wicked brother gLang Darma, who leaned heavily towards the nobles and Bon po and unleashed a reign of terror and indulged in anti-religious actions. All important posts were awarded to the conspirators and their friends. Consequently a fierce campaign against Buddhism ensued. He sealed the temples of Rampoche and Tsukla-Khang in Lhasa, the Samye monastery and many other religious centres. The Buddhist icons were removed and thrown out and the painstakingly translated texts were destroyed by fire. The monks fled for their lives. Several were caught, tortured and made to do humiliating tasks, while others were killed during fights. Those who remained were constrained to disown their religion and their priesthood. Many non-Buddhist tantrik teachers were welcomed from India, who interpreted the tantrik teachings literally, teaching people to freely indulge in the enjoyment of wine and women. Buddhist teachers were sent back to their countries and the translation of canonical texts was stopped. The Tibetans who had taken Buddhist vows were forced to renounce them or face death. Because of his severe anti-religious activities he came to be known amongst the Buddhists as 'Lang (Bull) Darma'. When his atrocities became unbearable, a courageous monk named Belgyi Dorje, killed him during a theatrical performance. Pretending to enact a traditional story, he danced in front of the king, holding a bow and arrow. Placing the arrow in the bowstring, Belgyi Dorje aimed it at the king, still pretending to be acting, and shot Lang Darma dead. According to Tibetan tradition, the killing was euphemistically characterized ... 'liberation', rather than killing, because Belgyi Dorje is said to have been motivated by compassion for the king, and not anger. Belgyi Dorje was concerned that Lang Darma, possessed by a demon, was creating vast amounts of negative karma for himself due to his persecution of Buddhism, and so he decided to 'liberate' the king from committing misdeeds in future, thus saving him from himself.

The successors of Darma were kings of no importance, putting an unceremonious end to the line of religious kings-Chosgyal. There was a severe disintegration of the body politic and Central Tibet remained fragmented by local hegemonies for the next 400 years—from AD 842 to AD 1254.

3

Bodhisattva—A Buddha to Be

BEFORE MOVING ON with the study of the impact of Buddhism on Tibet, it is imperative to pause and understand two major concepts, which are basic to the Tibetan form of Buddhism—Bodhisattva (Buddha to be) and Avalokitesvara (the enlightened one).

All religions have their archetypal figures, and mythologies worldwide describe the interaction between mortals and immortals, men and gods, because such things reflect the basic structures of the mind and therefore the problems common to people everywhere. The Bodhisattva deity is the most articulate in that it elucidates and connects both the worlds, the earthly and the heavenly, in one image and one body.

Bodhisattva literally means—one whose perfect essence or 'sattva', is perfect enlightenment or 'bodh'. A Bodhisattva is a Buddha to be, a 'being of enlightenment'. One who has attained the 'Paramitas' or perfections, has gone through the ten stages and is therefore qualified to enter Nirvana and become a Buddha, but prefers to remain a Bodhisattva. A Bodhisattva totally relies on the word of the Buddha. The interpretation of the concept of Bodhisattva differs in the two main divisions of Buddhism—Mahayana and Hinayana. In the former, the Bodhisattva is resolved to use his great powers for the benefit of all living beings in lower stages of development. He has, in all intents and purposes, reached the highest wisdom already, but he voluntarily postpones, indefinitely, his achievement of 'Nirvana' or Buddha-hood. In the Hinayana sect, he does not do this, but aims at full enlightenment as quickly and as directly as possible. He is called 'Arhant', in Hinayana tradition. In Mahayana, the heavens are occupied by innumerable Bodhisattvas who work for the welfare of all beings. They are constantly active in the service of all living things. They not only provide the ideals on which the believer, monastic or lay, should model himself, but also serve as potent sources of help in trouble. He is a person who seeks enlightenment not only for himself but for all living beings as well, devoting himself to the percepts—Four Wisdoms and Six Paramitas (perfections). The Bodhisattva ideal is the central aspect of Mahayana Buddhism.

Since Buddha-hood is almost as rare in Buddhism as is divinity in monotheistic religions, 'Arhantship' rather than Buddha-hood is the projected personal ideal in 'Nibbanic' Buddhism (Buddhism of Nirvana), i.e., Hinayana Buddhism. However, in Mahayana Buddhism, the ideal is not 'Arhant' but the Bodhisattva, who defers his entry into 'Nirvana', in order to help others in their quest for deliverance.

The entire practice of the Bodhisattva is classified under the 'Six Perfections', which are generosity, ethics, patience, effort, concentration and wisdom. Generosity is defined as the attitude of willingness to give away without a touch of miserliness, your own possessions, body, virtues and so forth. And the perfection of generosity is not with the aim of rooting out poverty in society but with the aim of developing a generous attitude. The Bodhisattva comes into being with the development of the 'Awakening Mind', the purely altruistic wish to achieve the state of a Buddha; and with his motivation, he then proceeds to engage in a way of life that is conducive to the realization of his goal. Altruism based on compassion and love is the basic theme of Buddhism. The qualities of love and compassion are the ultimate source of human happiness and our need for them lies at the very core of our being. The practice of compassion is not just a symptom of unrealistic idealism, but the most effective way to pursue the best interests of others. The great compassion is the prime cause of establishment of the Sakyamuni (prince of the Sakya tribe) Buddha as the embodiment of valid knowledge. The Buddha realizes that the cultivation of a compassionate mind for the sake of others' well-being is inevitable for him, as the immediate task before him is to liberate all beings from 'Samsara' (world). In order to carry out his mission successfully, Bodhisattvas undertake incessant practices and training for developing compassion. The Bodhisattva is so full of compassion that he always endeavours for the welfare of others and strives to relieve the suffering in beings. He earnestly wishes that the living beings, who are constantly suffering from miseries, should get rid of them. But before he desires to liberate the suffering beings from their miseries, he should first himself know the nature of the misery, its cause, its cessation and the way to its cessation, i.e. the fourfold truth. The Bodhisattva is reflected most archetypically in the Kwan-yin pledge. Kwan-yin is said to have been a Chinese princess who married a Tibetan king and converted him to Buddhism. The Kwan-yin is said to have taken this pledge:

'Never will I seek nor receive individual salvation; nor will I enter final peace alone; but forever and always will I strive for the redemption of every single creature from the bonds of conditioned existence.'

This noble utterance immediately reveals two things about the Bodhisattva. First the pledge can only be authentically taken by a very high being who cannot use speech in the degraded, careless fashion that we do in the making of claims and commitments cavalierly, and secondly the Bodhisattva commits himself to a central focus of thought not only for one life but for several lifetimes. The Bodhisattva has understood the full meaning of the verse of the 'Dhammapada' – the holy text of verses: 'All that we are, is the result of what we have thought: it is found on our thoughts', and he has taken on, in making the pledge, the highest ideal conceivable to humanity. For him such ideal thoughts are more real than 'Maya' or everyday facts of life. However, in this pledge of the Bodhisattva lies a paradox: the Bodhisattva sets for himself an ideal, which cannot ever be fully attained and yet he throws his whole being into its achievement with focussed interest, concern and total commitment unknown to an average man.

The 'Abhidharmakosha', a holy text, gives a fine description of the mentality of the Bodhisattva:

'But why do the Bodhisattvas, once they have taken the vow to obtain supreme enlightenment, take such long time to obtain it?'

Because supreme enlightenment is very difficult to obtain: one needs a vast accumulation of knowledge and merit, innumerable heroic deeds in the course of three immeasurable kalpas (eons).

One could understand that the Bodhisattva seeks for this enlightenment, which is so difficult to obtain, as if this enlightenment were his only means of arriving at deliverance. But this is not the case. Why then do they undertake such infinite labour?

For the good of others, because they want to become capable of pulling others out of this great flood of sufferings. But what personal benefit of others is in their denial of Nirvana for themselves?

It is true that men who are devoid of pity and who think only of themselves, find it hard to believe in the altruism of the Bodhisattva. But compassionate men do so easily. Do we not see that certain people, confirmed in the absence of pity, find pleasure in the suffering of others, even when it is not useful to them? As well one must admit that the Bodhisattvas confirmed in pity, find pleasure in doing good to others without any egoistic preoccupation. Do we not see that certain people, ignorant of the true nature of the conditioned Dharmas, which constitute their so-called 'self', do no longer consider these Dharmas as 'I' or 'Mine', growing in pitying solicitude for others and are ready to suffer a thousand pains for their solicitude'?

A Bodhisattva works for human beings whether or not they realize, understand or care. The basic characteristic of a Bodhisattva, in any level of spiritual attainment, is always looking to the true self-interest of the other. Thus the Bodhisattva sees that his own true self-interest is bound up in passionately serving others. For this the Bodhisattva must already have achieved a high state of spiritual knowledge, self-control, devotion and illumination.

In Buddhism in general, and particularly in the 'Great Vehicle' or Mahayana practice, the simple fact of being conscious of others' sufferings and difficulties is seen as a very beneficial inner attitude as this allows love and compassion to be born in us naturally. Love, joy, compassion and equanimity constitute the four 'immeasurables' that are the very core of Mahayana practice. Love is to wish for happiness among people in the present and the future, compassion wishes to alleviate others' suffering, equanimity is the exercise of looking at all beings in the same way as we look at our own mother. These can be developed by having affection for all beings. Loving affection can be developed by recognizing all beings as having been our mothers in previous births, remembering their kindness and wanting to repay their kindness out of gratitude. When these four attitudes penetrate our mind and guide our way of thinking, talking and acting, this is called Bodhichitta: 'Bodhichitta' implies the compassionate wish to achieve Buddha-hood for the sake of others. These 'immeasurables' can be achieved by understanding the inherent instability and transcience of relationships and their dependence on actions and their effects. Since all these practices or realizations are interdependent, therefore concentrating on only one of them is insufficient. When the four 'immeasurables' dwell within us, we come naturally to avoid all that could harm others and are led to accomplish their benefit.

Someone who has all the intelligence and practicality of the world but lacks love and compassion can never truly accomplish anything beneficial for others. But one who has love and compassion deeply within himself will accomplish benefit for others in everything he does. In the words of Santideva:

'I am not angry
About a sickness that makes me suffer.
Why therefore should I have anger for others,
they too are under the influence of conditions.
Understanding the lack of freedom
within others, when they are
aggressive, prevents us from rejecting
them in return. On the contrary
our compassion will wish to help
them now and in the future.'

In one of his lectures the Dalai Lama said. 'If Buddha achieved enlightenment for the sake of all sentient beings, then he achieved it for all of us and in this sense we are equal.' For a Bodhisattva altruistic aspiration is for the sake of everyone. Every sentient being is a means by which one can develop meritorious powers of love, compassion and wisdom. Others are far more important than oneself and from this one can learn to cherish others far more than oneself. We tend to blame others for everything which is wrong because we cannot bear to recognize the true culprit, i.e. selfishness. The root of all disturbing emotions, which leads us to act negatively and the source of all our sufferings, is our misconception of the self and our exaggerated self-concern. Unless we rid ourselves of this misconception and of our egoism, we will never banish them completely; but even if we cannot get rid of them completely for the time being, we can stop their pervasive influence. The problem is that we and our disturbing emotions seem totally inseparable. Though these emotions seem an integral part of us, they are not. We see ourselves as quite substantial, solid and concrete, whereas we are like the reflection of the moon in the rippling water, undergoing constant change. This self-conception of ours is not in tune with the fact that people are created, that their minds and bodies depend upon causes and conditions and hence they are impermanent. This leads to adhering to the 'self', the 'I' (which is non-existent due to its impermanence) and hence to sufferings. By reflecting on the fact that a belief in the unsound concept ... of a solid and substantially existent self draws sentient beings into suffering-compassion is easily generated.

Santideva (santideva was an Indian master whose magnumopus—*Bodhicaryava Tara*—is highly revered and studied even today) points out that all our happiness comes from cherishing others and all our fears and misfortunes from cherishing self:

'All the joy the world contains
has come from wishing happiness for others.
All the misery the world contains
has through wanting pleasure for one-self.'

We have always been in search of personal happiness and have always tried to avoid suffering, but our quest has been unsuccessful. Bodhisattvas, however, put the concerns of others first and help us to forget ourselves. Quoting *(Conze-Perfection of Wisdom, Selected Sayings)*:

'For Bodhisattvas take pleasure in the wholesome practice of renouncing all their belongings, a Bodhisattva must cast away even his body and must renounce all that is necessary to life. He should react to danger with the thought: if those beings take away from me, all that is necessary to life, then let that be my gift to them. If someone should rob me of my life, I should feel no ill will, anger or fury on account of that.

Even against them I should take no offensive action, either by body, voice or mind. This will be an occasion to bring the act of giving, morality and patience to greater perfection and I will get nearer to complete enlightenment. When I have attained enlightenment, I will act and behave in such a way that in my Buddha field, wildernesses infested with robbers will in no way whatsoever either be, or even be conceivable.' This constitutes an incarnation of a Bodhisattva.

In D.T. Suzuki's (D.T. Suzuki is one of Japan's foremost authority on Zea Buddhism) partial translation of, and commentary on, the 'Gandavyuha Sutra' (a holy text) there are remarks made about what assists one in becoming a Bodhisattva. One element that is considered important is the cultivation of good friends (kalyanmitra). Suzuki implicitly recognizes that we must ask the question, 'What constitutes a good friend?' Those who are friends with us because they can use and exploit us for their own purposes cannot be counted as good friends. Nor can those be called friends who are friendly to us because of a kind of a neurotic dependence, that is, who attach themselves to us because they find a lack in themselves and need us to fill it. Plato in his dialogue, 'The Symposium', has Aristophanes say that at some time in a man's past, he was slit in half so each one of us is only half a whole human being and thus we rush about the world desperately clinging to various people we hope are our other half. This mystic characterization very well captures the substance of most human relationships. There is a kind of desperation about them to a kind of fulfil their needs, which suggests that neither party is a whole independent being, a true individual on his own.

If a good friend cannot be he who exploits, nor he who has needs, then he must be the one who can give and uplift his friend. A good friend leaves each one he meets with a little clearer intimation, a little stronger feeling of the essential nobility. Hence two or more good friends working together may form a powerful current that elevates both towards enlightenment. A good friend can of course do this only by recognizing the higher values within himself and thereby recognizing the higher values within others.

A good friend, then, is one who sees good in others always. Infact he sees so many possibilities for the good, that he is actually capable of handling judgments for others' limitations. Good friends working together form an earthly reflection of the brotherhood of the Bodhisattvas, who work for all beings.

A Bodhisattva takes many vows, among which the following ten are paramount:

(1–6) To abstain from violating discipline, from being haughty, from anger, from envy, from jealousy and from attachment to material things.

(7) To practice the four acceptances—charity, loving words, benefiting deeds and working together in order to help others and to abide in non-attachment.

(8) To free all beings from sufferings.

(9) To protest against violation of discipline.

(10) To keep the True Law.

But the 'Diamond Sutra' tells us that while the Bodhisattva vows to save every being, the Bodhisattva at the same time recognizes that there are no beings to be saved. What kind of view of the universe must the Bodhisattva then have? The Bodhisattva must then have a profound realization of the essential unity of all things and must see that this unity is reflected on every plane of existence. Hence, while we see, on the worldly plane, fragmented consciousnesses, the Bodhisattva sees the thread that unites all the consciousnesses, and hence all beings, into one group. And now coming to the question of the agony or suffering of the Bodhisattva. Since the Bodhisattva has the option of entering into 'Nirvana' and renounces it, we are inclined to think that he suffers. But he sees 'Nirvana' as a flight from mankind. The desire for it may be the subtlest form of that very sense of separateness that he believes in the origin of suffering in the universe. On the other hand, in renouncing 'Nirvana', he definitely takes on the limited forms of embodiment and of action on the human plane. Even if he chooses to remain discarnate, he nevertheless must occupy some vehicles, no matter how refined, and thereby limit his own modes of operation. Thus the Bodhisattva's primordial sacrifice is that of impelling his consciousness into some level of incarnation. This is a part of the cause of the suffering of a Bodhisattva. But his suffering is not the suffering of ignorance. He has voluntarily and with full self-awareness, renounced 'Nirvana' and engaged himself in the activity of saving sentient beings from misery. We, on the other hand suffer because we do not understand the conditions in which we must operate or because we can't get what we want or because others do not do what we desire; we are not suffering the suffering of the Bodhisattva.

There is another kind of suffering, both more tragic and more noble, than the one a Bodhisattva undergoes. That is helplessly watching others engage in activities, the general nature and consequences of which he knows, and yet he cannot interfere because others have to learn for themselves. The Bodhisattva must stand by and watch countless humans destroy themselves and one another, committing useless acts of physical and psychological violence, incarnation after incarnation, since he cannot interfere with the Karma of others. He stands as a witness to seemingly perpetual personal degradation and yet sees the purity of our Buddha nature.

The Bodhisattva must know exactly what he is doing and must continue doing it because he regards it as that very thing for which he has been incarnated. However much material good a man may achieve for others, if he has done it for the sake of his career, for personal feelings or from a desire to upset existing regimes, then that does not make him a Bodhisattva. A Bodhisattva may enter politics, if he regards it as the best means of achieving his aim, but the majority work quietly and inconspicuously in less ethically dangerous fields. Only the highest can, with impunity enter public life. And it is not by their achievements but by their spiritual qualities that they are known, by the feeling that they arouse by their presence and by the example of their lives which are lived on a plane above the ordinary that they are known for. The Bodhisattva himself, is striving after higher development for himself, still trying to attain complete self mastery so that finally he is able to break all shackles, which hold him back from Buddha-hood and enlightenment.

The Bodhisattva is then much more than a human being with an exceptionally generous heart. In striving to achieve an ideal himself, a Bodhisattva becomes an ideal for us, for his life can be reflected in our lives. If the Buddha-nature is to be found in every man then the Bodhisattvas help is not merely a matter of abstract goodwill or localized assistance but in part comes through his standing as a model or archetype for all human activities and relations. The potential ability inherent in all to achieve enlightenment or to become Buddhas is called Buddha-nature. It is the intellectual basis of man, his nature or quality, by the existence of which he can attain Buddha-hood. The fundamental teaching of Buddhist philosophy is the fact that complete liberation is possible from the bonds of existence. The confusion and darkness of 'samsaric' (worldly) existence can be totally cleared and enlightenment can be attained through devotion. This ability to achieve, release and illuminate is inherent in all beings. The possibility of its realization may be remote and difficult but its presence in everyone is admittedly there. It is this potentiality which is called Buddha-nature. So long as Buddha-nature is not realized, man goes on taking physical forms according to his karma and his mind will remain locked up in the cage of individuality. The individual has to feel intuitively about the Buddha-nature hidden in him and make the necessary effort to see it and know it. When the egoistic individuality ceases to make its appearance, Buddha-nature is revealed as the only immutable reality.

The Buddha-nature is present in varying degrees in individuals and this variability has been explained by the Buddha himself: Buddha says that in a pond of lotuses, there are some that are born in water and remain totally immersed in water: others reach the surface, whereas a few of them rise out of the water, undefiled by the latter. In the same way there are people with much dirt in their eyes, with dull faculties, bad dispositions etc., while there are others with acute faculties, good dispositions etc.; the fact that everyone possesses

Buddha-nature is clearly implied here. In the Mahaparinirvana Sutra (a holy text) it is stated, 'Buddha-nature in all beings dwells permanent and unalterable throughout all transmigrations, ever ready to develop itself, no sooner than the opportunity presents itself'. But in some people it is totally hidden and their chances of realizing it are very remote, like the lotuses that remain in darkness inside the waters. Their karma is so heavy that they do not see that light is available somewhere. Hence they are said to have much dust in their eyes. Based on the realization of the Buddha-natures, people have been classified into three types in some Buddhist schools: according to this classification, the first type do not possess Buddha-nature by resolution and hence do not reach Nirvana. The second type are unresolved regarding it and hence have the possibility of attaining it by exertion. The third comprise those who have it by resolution and hence they are the real saints or Bodhisattvas. For the realization of our inherent Buddha-natures it is essential to put ourselves in others' situations and consider them as our equals in every sense. This equalizing and exchanging the self is a five-way process: first is the ability to express in action the insight that we and the others are the same. The second is to examine the faults of selfishness from different angles. Third is to recognize the great benefits of cherishing others. The fourth is the actual practice of exchange. Finally to strengthen love and compassion, we take on the sufferings of others and give away our happiness. The aim in cultivating an altruistic intention is to become less selfish. Although the powers of the celestial Bodhisattva are supernormal, every living being is considered a potential Bodhisattva. The awakening to the thought of enlightenment transforms the ordinary human being into a Bodhisattva.

Besides the qualities of love and compassion which are stressed by Buddhist morality as necessary condition for becoming a Bodhisattva, the towering figure of Buddha is a ubiquitous model for the Buddhist. Although the Buddha cannot directly save the others, he attempted to achieve the same end indirectly by sharing his wisdom with them. When he attained enlightenment, he could have entered Nirvana directly but due to his compassion for mankind, he deferred his deliverance, so that by revealing his discovery, to others, they too might learn the way to salvation.

No word such as Bodhisattva, or any word composed of similar elements, occurs in the voluminous Vedic literature and the same is true of early Hinduism and Jainism. This leads to the tentative though unprovable conclusion, that the concept of the Bodhisattva, in its original form, arose in a purely Buddhist framework, without influence from the outside during its inception. The idea of mercy or 'karuna', which was an ancient Buddhist concept, was thus concretized in the personification of the Bodhisattva, who would sacrifice everything, his own personal happiness and his own merits, for the sufferings of humanity. He would continue to bring solace in countless births and rebirths.

Bodhisattva (literally a man who strives after perfect wisdom) is a name attached to the Buddha in his formative status. 'Buddha' and 'Bodhisattva' have made a co-relative development in the history of Buddhism. Originally the appellation 'Bodhisattva' meant Gautama in his stage of striving, that is, Gautama in the period after his departure from home and before the attainment of Buddha-hood. In time the name was also applied to Gautama, before his departure from home. When the 'Jatakas' (tales of the Buddha in his previous existences), came about, Bodhisattva represented Gautama in his previous existences. And when it came to be believed that there were former, future and present Buddhas, and Buddhas in ten-quarters of the world, it naturally followed that there were a large number of Bodhisattvas too.

It thus follows about a Bodhisattva that he is distinguished by tremendous amount of suffering and toil which he undergoes for the sake of others due to his great compassion and heroism in working for the salvation of mankind. The Buddha has said that Bodhisattvas need not be concerned with many aspects of the path; they neeed not practice many other things. It is by one practice alone that Buddha-hood will be in the palm of your hand. That one practice is great compassion, meaning the desire to become enlightened in order to liberate other sentient beings. A Bodhisattva possesses 32 extraordinary qualities and 80 special marks of distinction on his body. However, his most profound hallmark is his great compassion. In the words of Santideva, 'All other paths pass the way, the paths of compassion leads to'.

4

Avalokitesvara—The Compassionate One

THE CULT OF THE AVALOKITESVARA was introduced in Tibet a little earlier than seventh century BC when the great Tibetan ruler Sron-btsan-gampo was proclaimed as being the incarnation of the Avalokitesvara. In India Avalokitesvara was worshipped from the third to the twelfth century and became popular in China in the eighth century. Avalokitesvara was an important figure in the Indian Buddhist pantheon, whose following had come to extend throughout much of Asia, long before Buddhism ever became established in Tibet. In India Avalokitesvara is regarded as God; 'Lokite' means 'The Lord of the World' and Avalokitesvara means 'Transcendent Protector'. In Tibet the Dalai Lama is believed to be his incarnation. As he possesses many aspects of Hindu Gods (especially of Shiva) Avalokitesvara is probably a development of the Indian 'Bhakti' devotion. However, there are efforts to connect him with 'Sumana' of Sri lanka, 'Istar' of Babylon and 'Apollo Patareus' of Asia Minor too. In China he is the most popular Bodhisattva and supreme saviour of the beings from evils of existence as well as from other calamities. The Chinese know him as

'Kuan-Shih-yin' or simply 'Kwan-yin'; the Koreans pronounce the Chinese name as K(w)anseum and in Japan he is known as K(w)an-an-se-on or simply 'Kannon'. In China the 'Kwan-yin' is often pictured carrying a child in his arms and for this reason is often known to be a female. Hence the Bodhisattva Avalokitesvara may be incarnate as a man or woman.

Avalokitesvara is the most prominent deity of the northern school of Buddhism—the Mahayana. There are numerous interpretations of Avalokitesvara. The name maybe regarded as originating from two Sanskrit words: 'Avalokita'—he who looks down upon the world with compassion and 'Isvara'—the lord. This looking down in compassion is from the 'Tusita' heaven, where Avalokitesvara is regarded to dwell. It is equally possible, however, that 'Avalokita' means 'he who is looked upon' (for help). Avalokitesvara therefore represents an essential aspect of Buddha-nature—compassion. With the compassion of the Avalokitesvara is linked his miraculous power to help human beings, when they call upon him in times of difficulty or distress. In his cosmic aspect Avalokitesvara is the sovereign lord of the universe; hence he possesses absolute power to protect men from natural disasters such as storms; on the other hand, to grant fertility to childless women. He is the embodiment of mercy and compassion. He goes through much suffering, assumes various forms of Buddha—arhant and even an animal, and goes everywhere including heaven and hell to save all beings, to free them from pain and evil passions, to bestow on them offerings and other blessings and to lead them to the 'pure land'.

As Mahayana Buddhism spread, the worship of Avalokitesvara as a saviour appealed to the devotion of the masses and helped to establish Buddhism as a religion of the people. In the minds of the Mahayana devotees, two of the most important characteristics of Avalokitesvara were his compassion or mercy and his assumption of different forms according to the needs and dispositions of people in various places and various ages. The idea of his continual rebirths and his assumption of different forms in different times and places allowed the absorption of previous gods, saints, religious leaders and heroes into the cult of the Avalokitesvara. The monks could say to the people that their gods were in reality Avalokitesvara. This gave popular Buddhism ready acceptance. The acceptance of the dharma of the Buddha then became a fulfilment of the ancient aspirations and religious traditions, rather than a turning away from the past to something new and foreign. Kings and heroes came to be looked on as incarnations of Avalokitesvara. The process also enabled new deities brought into a Buddhist environment to be accepted as manifestations of Avalokitesvara.

Some Tibetan historians have assigned the inception of the Avalokitesvara cult in Tibet to the reign of Sron-btsan-gampo. At first the religious king Gampo, taught the 'Creation and consummation of Mahakarunika' and other percepts at length and there were many who practiced them too. It was from this that the custom spread throughout Tibet and Kham, of praying to 'Arya Avalokitesvara' and reciting the six-syllable mantra – *om mani padme hum*. In addition to acting as a teacher in his own right, the king is said to have encouraged and sponsored establishment of shrines and images, as well as the translation of the fundamental texts of the Indian Avalokitesvara tradition into Tibetan. The spiritual activity begun by Gampo was continued on a vast scale by his descendant Khri Srong.

The early Buddhists, to some degree had believed in the eternal principle of Buddha-hood as evidenced in their conception of other Buddhas having preceded Sakyamuni in the past and also of a future Buddha. Around the beginning of the 'Kushan Period', or before, the Mahayanists devised a complex system of successive simultaneous Buddhas, some appearing in human form and others being transcendent. In course of time Mahayana Buddhists came to deify the Buddha who was conceived as the timeless Absolute. To bridge the distance between the transcendent realms and this world, the Buddhas have active emanations called Bodhisattvas.

Various accounts in numerous holy texts speak extensively of the fact that Buddhas and Bodhisattvas consciously take rebirth for the good of the living beings. According to the 'Hundred Thousand Sayings of the King' and the 'Karandavyhua Sutra', Amitabha, the Buddha of Infinite Light, who reigns in the Land of Bliss (Dewachen), one day conceived that in order to help beings a deity in the form of a young man should be manifested. His right eye then emitted a beam of white light that took the form of 'Chenrezig' or Avalokitesvara. He saw the necessity of having a deity in the form of a young woman and a beam of green light sprang from his left eye giving birth to Tara.

Having being born from the eye of Amitabha, the young man miraculously appeared on a lotus. In those days there was a king called Sublime Kindness (Zangpochok) in the Land of Bliss (Dewachen). A thousand queens were his companions, but he had no son. This was his great regret, and he fervently wished for the coming of an heir. In order to fulfil his wish, he gave much of his wealth to the dharma and, on his shrine, presented many offerings to the Buddhas and the 'Three Jewels'. He regularly sent a servant to the Lotus Lake, lying not very far from the palace to bring back fresh flowers for the shrine. One day when the servant went to pick flowers, he saw a wonderful child seated on the heart of a lotus. He immediately ran to the palace and reported this to the king.

The king thought that his prayers had been fulfilled; the miraculous child could be none other than the son for whom he had wished so much. He went to the Lotus Lake with his entourage to invite the young man to come and live with him. This boy appeared to be 16 years old, was adorned with silks and jewels and was ceaselessly saying, 'Poor beings! Poor beings!'

The boy then came to live in the palace. The king called him 'Heart of Lotus' (Padmai Nyingpo) because of the circumstance surrounding the boy's discovery.

The king Sublime Kindness wanted to know from where the young man came. He therefore went to see Amitabha and asked him whose emanation 'Heart of Lotus' was and what was his true name.

'This child is an emanation of the activity of all the Buddhas', answered Amitabha. 'He is the one who accomplishes the benefit of all beings, the one who makes joyful the heart of all the Buddhas. His name is "Chenrezig" – The Noble Sovereign. The help that this well-born son brings to beings will be as vast as space.'

When Chenrezig later looked at beings with compassion, he saw that they were covered with many karmic veils formed by the influence of desire, aversion, blindness, jealousy and pride. Thus their sufferings were innumerable. He saw all of that and a tear dropped from each of his eye. Tara appeared from the tear that fell from his right eye and goddess Lhmo Trulnyerchen appeared from the tear that fell from his left eye. The two deities said to him, 'Do not be scared. We will help you with your mission to benefit beings'. Then suddenly they melted again into his eyes.

While he was in the presence of Amitabha, Chenrezig thought, 'As long as there is even one being who has not attained awakening, I will strive for the benefit of all. And if I break this promise, may my head and body split into a thousand pieces'.

Amitabha understood his thought and told him, 'This promise is excellent. All the Buddhas and myself, having taken such commitments, attained awakening for the benefit of all. I will help you to accomplish that which you have promised'. Chenrezig's body then emitted six beams of light that produced emanations whose destiny was to act for the benefit of all in each of the six realms of being: humans, gods, demi-gods, animals, hungry ghosts and hell beings.

He thus worked for many 'kalpas' (eons). Then one day, he looked with the eye of knowledge from the top of Mount Meru, to see if the number of beings in the 'samsara' (world) had diminished. Alas he saw that they were still numerous.

He was very sad. Being discouraged, he thought, 'I do not have the capability to help beings; it is better that I rest in Nirvana'. This thought contradicted his promise and he burst into a thousand pieces and felt intense suffering.

Amitabha, by the power of his grace, reconstructed the body of Chenrezig. He gave him eleven faces and a thousand arms, similar to the thousand spokes of a universal monarch's wheel and a thousand eyes, symbolic of the thousand Buddhas of the present 'kalpa'. Chenrezig could henceforth help the beings in this form as well as with his other forms acquiring two or four arms. Amitabha asked Chenrezig to retake his promise with still more vigour than before and then transmitted to him the six-syllable mantra: *om mani padme hum*.

The Bodhisattva Avalokitesvara has been assingned to Tibet by the Buddha himself. This is authenticated by the following passage from the Great Chronicle of Mani Kabum (later part of the twelfth century) addressed to Avalokitesvara by the dying Buddha Sakyamuni – 'There are none left to be trained by me. Because there are none for me to train. I will demonstrate the way of Nirvana to inspire those who are slothful to the doctrine and to demonstrate that what is compounded is impermanent. The snowy domain to the north Tibet is presently a domain of animals, so even the word "human beings" does not exist there – it is filled with darkness. And all who die there turn not upwards but, like snowflakes falling on a lake, drop into the world of evil doctrines. At some time in the future when that doctrine declines, you O future Bodhisattva, will train them. First the incarnation of the Bodhisattva will generate human beings who will require training, then they will be brought together (as disciples) by material goods. After that bring them together through the doctrine. It will be for the welfare of living beings'.

From a variant translation of the Pundarika Sutra, we get another fascinating tale of how Buddha deputed Avalokitesvara to serve Tibet and its people:

At the time when the teacher was sitting in the bamboo forest, a ray of five colours emanated from the circle of hair between his eyebrows and went to the kingdom of snows in the north. Seeing this, the Bodhisattva 'Sarva-Nirvana-VishKambhin', smiled and asked the reason for this. The blessed one bestowed these words:

'Son of good family, in the kingdom of snows, which is a barbarian country full of many demons, like a country which has never been converted to Buddhism by any of the Buddhas of the three times – in that country, in future, the holy religion will rise like the sun. It will spread and become extensive. The living beings (there) will be set on the path of enlightenment which leads to salvation. The holy Avalokitesvara will be the spiritual guide who will convert that barbarian country.' Sarva-Nirvana-VishKambhin asked, 'Who is he?' The Buddha replied, "At the time when the holy god Avalokitesvara was performing the deeds of Bodhisattva, he uttered a prayer in the presence of a thousand Buddhas saying, "May I set the living beings, difficult to convert, who are in the barbarian kingdom of the snows, which has not been trodden by the feet of any Buddha of the three times, on the path of enlightenment which leads to salvation! May that barbarian country be the land converted by me! May I be like (the cause of) the defeat of the spirits, demons and other such living beings (who are there)! May I be like a guide for the salvation of the world! May I be like a lamp to remove the darkness! May all the teachings taught by the Buddhas of the three times and all the Tathagatas spread into the barbarian country, extend and remain there for a long time! May the living beings (of that country) hear the name of the Three Jewels, take refuge in them acquire bodies in the paradise of fortunate beings and enjoy the holy religion!"'

In accordance with this prayer, when the teacher was considering his imminent entry into Nirvana and leaving the task of liberating living beings to Avalokitesvara the Bodhisattva Avalokitesvara went to the kingdom of Kusinagara, bowed his head (at the feet of the Buddha) bent his right knee on the ground and said, 'your feet have not trodden the kingdom of snows in the north. It is unprotected by your words. Remain in this world for the sake of these'. The blessed one bestowed these words:

'The kingdom of snows in the north is, at present, a kingdom of animals. There is not even a trace of human beings there. In the black darkness, everything is dead. But as snow falls on the lakes of the worlds of evil ones, there will be a living world there. At that time, in the future, O Bodhisattva, it will be converted by you. At first having been reincarnated as a Bodhisattva, protect the human world of your disciples. Then gather together your followers by giving them goods. Then gather them together by religion.'

Avalokitesvara is a well-known figure in Buddhist texts such as Prajnaparamitahridya (The Heart of Transcendent Wisdom or Heart Sutra) where Avalokitesvara represents supreme compassion and 'Sariputra' represents wisdom and they are having a discussion which is said to be the word of the Buddha.

The Avalokitesvara – GunaKarandaVyuha (The Exhausted Description of the Basket of the Merits of Avalokitesvara) is entirely devoted to the praise of Avalokitesvara and his mission of mercy towards suffering beings in all of the worlds. This text opens with a salutation to Avalokitesvara, the great being, the

Bodhisattva, the great compassionate one. It describes how he descends to various hells, to bring solace to those suffering there and how he assumes different forms in different ages to help people in distress.

The Saddharma Pundarika gives even a more detailed description of the quality of Avalokitesvara. If the living in any realm must be saved the Bodhisattva Avalokitesvara appears and preaches to them the Law.

The larger Sukhavati Vyuha, which was translated from Sanskrit into Chinese for the first time in the second century AD, contains the earliest direct literary reference to Bodhisattva Avalokitesvara. The following passages (translated by Max Mueller in 1894) emphasize the compassionate nature of the Boddhisattva: 'There rises the Buddha-son, he is indeed the mighty Avalokitesvara and says: "What is the reason there, O Bahgavat (Amitabha), what is the cause that thou smilest, O Lord of the world!"'

'Explain this, for thou knowest the sense, and art full of kind compassion, the deliverer of many living beings. All beings will be filled with joyful thoughts, when they have thus heard this excellent and delightful speech.'

'And the Bodhisattvas who have come from many worlds to Sukhavati (Land of Bliss) in order to see the Buddha, having heard it and having perceived the great joy, will quickly inspect this country.'

'And beings come to this noble country, to obtain miraculous power, divine eye and divine ear, they remember their former births and know the highest wisdom.'

Amitabha then responds by saying that Avalokitesvara's description of what happens to beings who, come to his 'Buddha country', corresponds precisely to his own prayer to their well being:

'[If] beings having any way whatever, hear my name [they] should forever go to my country. And this, my excellent prayer has been fulfilled and beings having come here from many worlds into my presence, never return from here, not even for one birth.'

A full chapter is devoted to Avalokitesvara in the Saddharma Pundarika, which further emphasizes the Bodhisattvas response to those who find themselves in states of calamity or in mind-sets unconducive to spirituality.

Apart from Sukhavati Vyuha and Saddharma Pundarika Sutras, another early text where Avalokitesvara is associated with Amitabha is the Amitayur-dhyna Sutra. This gives significant information of Bodhisattva Avalokitesvara. According to this text, his abode is in the Buddhaland of 'Sukhavati' (Land of Bliss), where he is seen attending on Amitabha with another Bodhisattva. Those who meditate upon him, will not only be safe from any calamity but will also gain access to the paradisial Buddhaland. The text says that just hearing his name will enable one to obtain immeasurable happiness.

In stories and in images Avalokitesvara is often shown carrying a deer-skin on his back. This symbol is used because the deer is a compassionate animal and it does not kill other creatures, but lives on a vegetarian diet. Here Avalokitesvara appears as a sage, as in the Indian tradition where sages often carry their seats on their shoulders when they are travelling, and when they want to sit down they simply spread this on the floor and sit on it. In this particular case, the deer-skin symbolizes harmlessness or the act of compassion.

On top of Avalokitesvara's crown one sees the figure of Amitabha. This is because compassion must also have the attribute of wisdom and clarity, that Amitabha represents. And one also often finds Avalokitesvara portrayed as having a thousand arms, which symbolize his innumerable activities. The story about Avalokitesvara which relates how he took a vow to save all sentient beings in that very lifetime; he did whatever he could and then went up and looked around. He saw that even more innumerable beings than before were suffering. At this point he was at the verge of breaking his vow, as he felt that he could not help anyone anymore. This is compassion without wisdom, compassion without knowing. It is also compassion with ambition, a one faced compassion. And this is one of the reasons why Avalokitesvara is often shown with a figure of Buddha above his head, which means that compassion must be without ambition. It must also be ever growing. As long as there are more sentient beings and as long as there is more to be done, his compassion also increases. Therefore the act of compassion, the act of Avalokitesvara is never ending.

That is the basic meaning of Avalokitesvara. Of course there are variations, such as 'Kesarpani', 'the eleven-headed Avalokitesvara', 'The four-armed Avalokitesvara', 'Cintamani' and many other variations which are to be found in different scriptures and iconographies. Nevertheless they all stem from one source – the concept of Avalokitesvara as representing compassion. He is not only a Bodhisattva, he is a 'Mahasattva' or great being – the great Sattva. Nobody can become a Sattva until he has fully developed compassion. Therefore it is stated in many of the Sutras, Shastras and Tantras, that compassion is the companion of wisdom. Wisdom has depth and clarity, but it also needs to act. And that action is a perpetual forward movement. It never turns back having lost its purpose but goes on continuously, like the travelling of light.

The Avalokitesvara is not just a mythical concept, or a deity, it is not even a Bodhisattva, in the sense of somebody on the path of enlightenment but Avalokitesvara is a 'Mahasattva'. In the Saddharma Pundarika Sutra Avalokitesvara is the personification of the enlightened state of mind. So Avalokitesvara is the awakened mind. But this awakened mind is not just highly intelligent or all-knowing but it also contains compassion, one of the most important aspects of the awakened state. In the definitive sense Avalokitesvara is the mind of great compassion of all the Buddhas, hence, the epithet, The Great Compassionate One.

Compassion does not mean being compassionate to a person, or being sympathetic, or collecting charity – one has to go beyond this. Compassion or 'karuna', in Tibet, is known as the Noble Heart – the magnetic or moving quality of enlightenment. Hence, in addition to being an external symbol of compassion Avalokitesvara also symbolizes the compassion that exists within ones own heart, which is developed through true training. This Bodhisattva is often depicted with many arms expressing the different ways in which we must help other beings and with many heads, symbolizing the total awareness of meditation.

By finding true compassion within every situation, we can, in turn, find the wisdom and skilful means needed to help ourselves and others truly. We in a sense become the eyes and arms of the Avalokitesvara, helping all living things.

Whatever the situation, however hopeless it may seem, there is always an open door, always Avalokitesvara is present in all places, at all times, to help and serve:

'With all miraculous powers well endowed and widely skilled in knowledge of all things, in all the world, in all the quarters, there is not a place where 'Kannon' does not go. We need only ask' (Saddharma Pundarika).

Avalokitesvara is ultimately the great compassionate nature of all the Buddhas of the ten directions. This very nature, when manifested in physical emanations, according to the merit of the disciples, assumes the form of spiritual teachers, deities, Buddhas, Bodhisattvas, yogis, religious protectors and so forth. In human form, it is manifest as ordained novices and 'bhikshus'; and as laymen such as householders, kings and ministers and so forth, besides this it assumes even the forms of birds, animals, boats, bridges, etc., to help sentient beings in the most appropriate way.

This ultimate compassionate nature or Avalokitesvara is known in Tibetan as 'Chenrezig' – Chenrezig is the Tibetan term for the male form of Avalokitesvara. Literally translated, Chenrezig means 'glancing eye' or 'he who sees all sentient beings'. He does not move, he merely sees or observes and he never makes a mistake. He just looks in all directions and prepares for the next compassionate act. Chenrezig is both, the divine manifestation as well as an essence, with one not excluding or contradicting the other. The appearance of Chenrezig is the symbol of his essence and it is through this appearance we can approach the essence of Chenrezig. Chenrezig is within us because love and compassion are not qualities added to the mind, these qualities are part of the awakened state even if for the moment, this state exists only as a potential for us.

Saying that Chenrezig is the ultimate nature of the mind does not negate his form manifestation. The essence expresses through an appearance. Chenrezig exists on the level of definitive meaning and also on the level of literal meaning where he appears in the form of the deity by which he is usually known. He is the visible expression taken by all Buddhas to help us activate the love and compassion that are presently only a potential in us and to reveal the ultimate Chenrezig in ourselves. Even his name expresses his nature; each syllable that composes it in Tibetan has a meaning:

– Chen means eye
– re gives an idea of continuity
– zig means to look

Therefore Chenrezig is the one who 'continually looks upon all beings with the eye of compassion'. As a mother always looks after her child with an unwavering care and tries her best to provide all possible benefits, assistance and protection from all faults and harm, so does the great Avalokitesvara, look after sentient beings at all times and in all situations, with his unwavering eye of compassion, trying to liberate them from all faults and sufferings and place them in the state of virtue and happiness. If Chenrezig is the male aspect of Avalokitesvara, the feminine aspect of Avalokitesvara is the six-syllable mantra – *om mani padme hum*. This represents the sound or movement of Avalokitesvara – something which moves, something which goes forward. So the sound represents the feminine part of Avalokitesvara. The male part is the compassionate thought, stillness, the deep-rooted one, revered in Tibetan tradition as Chenrezig.

The mantra *om mani padme hum* is the sound manifestation coming from emptiness; it is the authentic sound of emptiness. The first syllable of the mantra, *om*, represents the 'form body' of a Buddha and the last syllable, *hum*, represents 'truth body'. *mani* means 'wish fulfilling gem', symbolizing the pure wisdom that has realized emptiness. The vowel E at the end of the word *padme* has been described as a call to someone. It is essentially a short symbolic supplication to Avalokitesvara, which says 'O Supreme Avalokitesvara you have attained the two bodies of a Buddha through the dual path of wisdom and method indicated by the Jewel and lotus you hold, please lead all sentient beings to attain the two bodies of the Buddha as you have done'.

Mantras are very often the names of Buddhas, Bodhisattvas, or deities. For instance, *om mani padme hum* is a way of naming Chenrezig. From an absolute point of view, Chenrezig does not have a name, but he is designated by names in the domain of the relative or literal meaning. These names are the vector of his compassion, grace and the strength of the wishes he makes for the benefit of beings. In this way the recitation of his name transmits these qualities of his mind. As we assimilate ourselves to our name and are one with it, similarly, on the relative level, the mantra is identical with the deity. They form a single reality. When we recite this mantra, we are in fact continually repeating the name of the Chenrezig.

This Buddhist magic formula *om mani padme hum* occupies a very important place in the everyday worship of the Tibetan people. Lots of money and time are expended by them in reproducing it on stones and paper.

Avalokitesvara therefore conclusively epitomizes compassion. It is not a remote figure in some exotic heaven, to which we might go in the next life. The religious veneration of the Avalokitesvara has become the 'cult of half of Asia'. The widespread popularity of this Mahayana Bodhisattva has been found in virtually every corner of Buddhist Asia; from the Hindukush in Central Asia, throughout the sub-continents of South Asia (India, Pakistan, Bangladesh, Nepal and Tibet), South-East Asia (Indonesia, Malaysia, Kampuchea, Thailand and Burma) and East Asia (China, Mongolia, Korea and Japan).

5
Schools and Masters of Tibetan Buddhism

FOR SOME TIME there was a lull in the conflict between aristocracy and monarchy but the conflict became sharp again during the reign of Ral pa chen, an ardent supporter of Buddhism. In him Tibetan aristocracy saw new threats to their existence and he was eventually murdered. gLang Darma's succession to the throne was manoeuvred by the aristocracy, in whose hands he played a puppet. However, his personal preference for Bon also prompted the aristocracy in enthroning him. The outcome of this religious turmoil was that Buddhism, as an organized religion, was almost effaced—at least from Central Tibet. This period in time is marked as the failure of the first propagation of Buddhism in Tibet. However, this age boasts of a major achievement too—the creation of the Tibetan language, which has over many centuries enabled the translation of the treasure of Indian Buddhist literature.

By the eleventh century, the state of affairs in Tibet, was causing great anxiety to the Tibetan scholars, which led them to invite the great Guru Atisa (whose original name was Dipamkara Srijnana) in 1042 from Nalanda, in India.

To the Tibetan Buddhists the story of Atisa is that of the final re-assertion of Buddhism in the land of the snow, after it went to pieces under the persecution of gLang Darma. From Atisa came not only the greatest impetus for Buddhist renaissance but also the right direction for purifying the doctrine, then surviving in Tibet. He was born into the royal family, but gave up the luxuries of home and wandered here and there studying tantrik and Mahayanist doctrines. Three of these years he spent on a course of mental training. Later on he lived in Afghanistan and Burma, thus gaining a varied experience before his thirtieth year when he joined monk-hood. When in later life, he filled the High Priest's office at the Vikramshila monastery his reputation for learning had spread widely. It was not until his sixtieth year, in AD 1039, that he came to west Tibet. He was about the last of the greatest Buddhist acharyas (teacher) of India, and though not the first, he is remembered in Tibetan tradition as by far the greatest of the teacher reformers of Tibet. By the middle of the eleventh century, the time of his departure for Tibet, Buddhism in India—especially in East India, its last Indian stronghold—was facing a serious crisis and was clearly on its decline.

According to Tibetan tradition, Atisa was born into a noble family in Bengal. He entered the religious life at an early age after experiencing a vision of the Buddha. During his early years he travelled around the Buddhist world to receive teachings. His first teacher was a tantrik yogin who initiated him into the Hevajra cycle, and he was mainly involved with non-monastic tantrik practises until in a dream Sakyamuni advised him to become a monk. He took ordination vows at the age of 29, in a monastery in Bodhgaya, the site of Buddha's enlightenment.

Atisa then immersed himself in the monastic curriculum current at that time, studying monastic discipline (vinaya), the perfection of wisdom literature, and tantrik texts.

Due to his incomparable learning and realizing capacities, he soon rose to prominence in the monastic university of Nalanda, where he was one of the four directors. He also taught at the Buddhist universities of Vikramshila and Bodhgaya, and was probably the most famous and revered Buddhist teacher of his day.

When he was advanced in years, a messenger sent by the Tibetan king Yeshe Od, visited him, presented him a sizeable amount of gold and asked him to journey to Tibet in order to reintroduce the Dharma there. Yeshe Od was an ardent Buddhist and was hence naturally worried over the condition of Buddhism, which during his time had fallen into perverse tantrik practices. He was at a loss to understand how far the tantrik practices, alleged to be Buddhist, really represented the doctrine. He was disgusted with the prevalent tantrik Buddhism. He doubted that the debased mysticism was Buddhism at all. With a view to reform the degenerate and corrupt Buddhism the king selected 14 intelligent and assiduous young men and six attendants, headed by Rin-chen-bzan-po, to proceed to India to find out how far the tantrik practices were to be accepted as genuinely Buddhistic. But little did Yeshe Od know that Indian Buddhism towards the end of tenth century was merging imperceptibly with tantrism! The study of classical works of Buddhism was fast deteriorating in India and Atisa himself had to leave India and go abroad for advanced studies in classical Buddhism. The king commanded them to bring with them any of the eminent Panditas (scholars) and accordingly the party of 21 men proceeded to their destination but out of these only three returned to Tibet, as the rest perished during the arduous travel through the mountainous terrain. Rin-chen-bzan-po was one of the three who returned but he himself came back to Tibet as an enthusiastic follower of some form of tantrism. Though he propagated a renewed, reformed form of veneration for tantras in Tibet, the less learned Tibetans remained rooted in sexual and sacrificial practices, which were deeply embedded in tantrism. Thus Yeshe Od's efforts to reform Buddhism could not be fully successful through the measures he took.

Atisa initially rejected the cache of gold and the request to come to Tibet, on the grounds that his teaching skills were required in India. Fearing that the gold was insufficient, Yeshe Od set about raising a much larger amount, in a hope that it would induce Atisa to accept the invitation. While trying to obtain funds from a neighbouring king, he was captured and imprisoned. The king demanded a ransom equal to Yeshe Od's weight in gold, but Yeshe Od advised his great nephew, Jangchub Od, not to pay it and instead to send the gold to Atisa. Jangchub Od reluctantly did so, with the result that Yeshe Od died in prison. This act of self-sacrifice is said to have been a factor in Atisa's eventual decision to travel to Tibet. In the life of Atisa, translated shortly after receiving the royal request, Atisa had a vision of Tara, his patron deity, who told him that if he travelled to Tibet his life would be shortened. Atisa was relieved by the news, assuming that it meant that he should not undertake the journey. He had advanced in age, and the journey to Tibet was long, difficult and dangerous. For these reasons, Atisa preferred to remain where he was. Tara then added that if he did go to Tibet, his visit would benefit many sentient beings and would cause the Dharma to flourish there. As a devout Mahayanist Atisa realized that he should choose the benefit of others over his own welfare, and so he agreed to go. Before he left he made a vow to the abbot of his monastery that he would return in three years. He is reported to have arrived in Guge, in Tibet, in 1042, at the age of 60.

His reputation in India gave him enormous personal authority in Tibet, with the result that his teachings were widely heeded. He composed several works on Buddhism for the benefit of the Tibetans, the most notable being his 'Lamp for the Path to Enlightenment'. In this work he brought together the two streams of scholastic Mahayana and tantra, both of which are viewed today by the Tibetan scholars as the complementary aspects of the Buddhist path.

Despite his intention to keep his promise and return to India, political factors prevented this, and he died in Tibet in 1054. During his years in Tibet, Atisa trained many disciples, several of whom became important figures in the development of Tibetan Buddhism. His instructions and influence led to the founding of the Kadampa order, the first school of Buddhism in Tibet, although the establishment of the clearly defined school was due primarily to the efforts of his disciple Dromdon (1008–1064). In 1057 Dromdon founded Reting monastery, which became the main seat of the order.

The Tibetan ruler, to whom Buddhist renaissance in Tibet owed so much, was a direct descendant of gLang Darma, who had made great efforts to annihilate Buddhism from Tibet. The first Tibetan king to have taken up the cause of Buddhism after gLang Darma, was Yeshe Od. The history of Tibetan

Buddhism after him is clear and the most important event in it is the coming of Atisa to Tibet.

In 1209 Tibet was invaded for the first time by a foreign power—by the army Changis Khan of Mongolia. Minyang was occupied due to which a few of the adjoining chieftains made peace with the Mongols. After the death of Changis Khan in 1240, his grandson Godan Khan invaded and captured most of Tibet and ruled it for 13 years. But in 1247, a major event occurred that furthered the cause of Buddhism in Tibet – Godan invited Sakya Pandita (Buddhist scholar from Sakya tribe) Kunga Gyeltsen to Mongolia and Godan and his community adopted Tibetan Buddhism. Kublai Khan, successor of Godan became disciple of Chosgyal Phagpa – the nephew of Sakya pandita Kunga Gyeltsan, who had accompanied his uncle to Mongolia. The brilliant and talented Phagpa impressed Kublai Khan. Kublai Khan invited Phagpa to the imperial court and appointed him the first imperial preceptor and gave him the authority over whole of Tibet. Thus Phagpa became the first lama sovereign of the country. The sovereignty of Tibet was restored once again, after a united Tibet was placed under the rule of lama Phagpa. This was the beginning of a new era of theocratic rule in Tibet. Phagpa, now called 'Don Chosgyal Phagpa' (Dharma king, The Protector of living beings), came back to Sakya in Central Tibet to consolidate the kingdom. Since then Tibet and Mongolia have had a special relationship—that of priest–patron or guru–shishya.

An important religious development in the fourteenth century began, which was to have a long range impact on the Tibetan political history, namely the great reformation movement led by Tsong Khapa (1357–1419), one of the greatest figures of Tibetan religious history.

A renowned scholar, meditator and philosopher, his written work contains a comprehensive view of Buddhist philosophy and practice that integrates sutra and tantra, analytical reasoning and yogic meditation. He was more importantly Tibet's greatest religious reformers, a devout Buddhist monk who dedicated his life to revitalizing Tibetan Buddhism and recapturing the essence of Buddha's teachings. Aiming his reform at the general decline in monastic morality prevalent in his time, Tsong Khapa, emphasized the adherence to disciplinary vows and stressed the importance of academic study, while rejecting many of the tantrik texts used by the other sectarian traditions as non-Buddhist works. These reformed teachings found a receptive audience in a disenchanted society, and within one decade the three major monasteries of the reformed sect in the Lhasa region were founded; Dga'-Idan in 1409, 'Bras-Sprungs in 1416 and Sera in 1419, the year of Tsong Khapa's death. The reformed order became known as the Dge-lugs-pa or Gelukpa (School of the Victorious) and is popularly referred to as the Yellow-Hat sect. For 70 years the High Priests of the Sakyas, the descendants of the Phagpa, the first lama soverign of Tibet, ruled as kings over a small part of the country. After the Sakya School dwindled, because of internal strife the Dge-lugs-pas or the Yellow-Hat lamas, came to be favoured by the powerful Mongol chieftain as spiritual leaders and later as temporal rulers of Tibet. When Altan Khan, ruler of Thumed Mongolia, met the third hierarch—Bsod-nams-rgya-mtso, he was convinced that the hierarch and he himself, were the reincarnations of the teacher Phagpa and his disciple Kublai

Khan respectively and so he immediately recognized the former as the veritable 'Tale' (i.e., Dalai, Tibetan rgya-mtso), meaning 'The Ocean'. Thereafter all hierarchs came to be recognized as Dalai Lamas. In 1447 the monastery of Bkra-Shis Ihun-po was founded near Shigatse by Dge'-dun grub-pa, a personal disciple of Tsong Khapa and the Yellow-Hat hierarch came to be revered in Tibetan Buddhism as the first Dalai Lama.

Tsong Khapa was born in the Tsongkha valley in the Amdo province of eastern Tibet. According to traditional biographies, his birth was the culmination of a process of spiritual development that began during a previous life, at the time of Sakyamuni (prince of the Sakya tribe) Buddha. As a young boy, he offered a crystal rosary to the Buddha, who presented him with a conch shell and told his attendant Ananda that in a future life the young boy would be born in Tibet. There he would found a great monastery and become one of the most influential figures in the spread of the Dharma in the 'Land of the Snows'. The Buddha then predicted that in his future life the young boy would be named, Sumatikirti (Sanskrit – Losang Drakpa).

Another prophesy is attributed to Padmasambhava, who is said to have predicted the birth of a great lama named Losang Drakpa. He said that Losang Drakpa would be born in the eastern part of Tibet, near China, that he would be considered to be an emanation of a Bodhisattva, and that he would attain the body of the Buddha; the fulfilment of both these prophesies would take place in 1357.

The event of Tsong Khapa's birth was presaged by auspicious events. Both his parents have been said to have had a series of dreams, prior to the birth of Tsong Khapa, which were indicative of the greatness of the unusual child which was to be born a year later. At age three the child was ordained and was given the name Kunga Nyingpo. At age seven he received novice vows and was given the name Losang Drakpa.

At an early age he began to travel widely throughout Tibet in order to find lamas who could teach him the Dharma. Following the footsteps of Atisa, he proved his brilliance early, studying with the best teachers from all sects. As he travelled, he discussed the tenets of Buddhism, engaged in oral debate with the greatest scholars of his day, and began to teach on his own. As a result the reputation of his remarkable intellect and meditational accomplishments began to spread. During his travels he met the lama whom he would later consider to be his greatest teacher, the Sakya master Rendwa. Rendwa quickly recognized that Tsong Khapa was a prodigy and believed that he learned as much from his student as his student learned from him. Traditional accounts of his life report that he quickly understood everything he was taught, memorized prodigious amounts of material and excelled in debate on all the subjects he studied. At the same time he was also engaged in tantrik practises of the highest order and was renowned both for his scholarship and his success in meditation.

At age 32 he began writing his most influential works. By this time he had a national reputation as an accomplished scholar of all aspects of Buddhist learning, and he began to synthesize his insights into written works that encapsulated his vision of how Buddhism ought to be practiced and conceived. One of his great early works is *The Golden Rosary of the Good Explanations*, a commentary on the 'Perfection of Wisdom' literature. In addition to his work with Buddhist philosophy, he concurrently dedicated himself to practising a wide range of tantrik meditations. He also became interested in Kalachakra practices, and he was concerned that the living tradition of Kalachakra was in danger of disappearing from Tibet. He collected the teachings and empowerments of Kalachakra from various lamas all over Tibet, and his efforts ensured that the tradition would be preserved. Kalachakra practices today are particularly important in the Gelukpa, or Yellow-Hat tradition.

One of his most important periods of meditative seclusion, he led a four-year retreat with eight of his most advanced disciples. In order to prepare himself, he began by doing three and a half million full length prostrations and one million eight hundred thousand mandala offerings. The stone floor on which he performed the prostrations has grooves worn into it and is still preserved today as a testament to the dedication of this great lama. After the retreat, he briefly considered visiting India but was dissuaded by another lama, since the lama felt that Tsong Khapa would be of greater benefit to sentient beings if he were to remain in Tibet and continue teaching there. As a result, he decided to compose treatises on the Buddhist path, the most important of them being his masterpiece—*The Great Exposition of the Stages of the Path*, which is still the central work on the Buddhist practice in Gelukpa monastic colleges. This work is based on Atisa's seminal work, *A Lamp for the Path to Enlightenment*. Tsong Khapa later composed a similar work on tantra, entitled '*The Great Exposition of Secret Mantra*', which is the basis of the Gelukpa or Yellow-Hat system of tantrik practice. In 1403 he composed his two famous synthesis of Buddhism—the Lam Rim and Ngag Rim.

One of the main goals of his teaching, writing and practise was the reform of Tibetan Buddhism. Part of his reform programme was the creation of a new order which stressed the importance of strict adherence to the vinaya or monastic discipline, the importance of comprehensive study of Buddhist thought, and reformed tantrik practice that accords with the vows of monks. This was important to Tsong Khapa, who was concerned that many of his tantrik contemporaries were involved in sexual practices that were incompatible with the monastic vows. These were mainly practitioners of highest yoga tantra. It was commonly thought that highest yoga tantra was the supreme of all tantrik sets and that it could not be practised by monks. Though he agreed that the highest yoga tantra is the supreme of tantrik practices, but Tsong Khapa also thought that it could be reconciled with a monastic lifestyle.

Tsong Khapa's followers were called Galdanpa after Galden (Ganden) Monastery, established by him near Lhasa in 1409. Along with Sera and Drepung monasteries, Ganden became the power base for the Gelukpa or Yellow-Hat and helped re-establish Lhasa as a centre of influence. The monastery was officially opened in 1409. Ganden later became a huge monastic complex, housing as many as 4,000 monks. Ganden, Drepung, and Sera became the three principal seats of power. They were ransacked by the Chinese army in 1959, and Ganden was bombed into rubble. All three monasteries have been rebuilt in India, where they continue the scholastic and meditative traditions established by Tsong Khapa.

Whoever became abbot at Ganden also became official head of the entire Gelukpa order. Tsong Khapa's illustrious disciple Gedun Truppa was posthumously regarded as the first Dalai

Lama and his lineage was to become the single most important within Buddhist hierarchy of Tibet. The Gelukpa or Yellow-Hat sect of the Dalai Lama was a group of reformists dedicated to cleaning up the abuses in the Tibetan monastic system. Emphasizing celibacy and scholasticism as prerequisites to advanced tantrik studies practices, visualizing them as returning to 'pure' Buddhism.

It is possible to distinguish nine schools of practice in Tibet, although over the course of time, four of them became dominant, each eventually establishing its own separate existence in its monasteries, retreat—centres, colleges and supporting lay communities. These four schools are – Nyingma, Sakya, Kagyu and the Gelug. For an understanding of the schools of Tibetan Buddhism, their development would have to be traced out of the activity of particular masters and their disciples. Buddha had given so many different practices to lead beings to enlightenment that clusters of gurus and disciples were able to specialize in only one particular set of teachings, for which perhaps they alone held the transmission. These schools hence represent the culmination of a long process of development carried on by the groups of gurus and their disciples, each group transmitting a series of instructions from the Indian inheritance.

The Nyingma School

The School of the Ancient Transmission Period in the eighth century, from the collaboration between Khri srong and the two Indian masters Shantirakshita and Padmasambhava, the lineages of teachings comprising the Nyingma tradition may be said to originate. The tantrik teachings of Padmasambhava are therefore especially important in the Nyingma School. The early practitioners belonging to the Nyingma school were the 'Ngakpas', or 'tantrik yogins', who mastered and preserved the oral transmission teachings of Guru Padmasambhava. They continued the practice of Buddhism right through the dark period of Tibet's history, between the ninth and the eleventh centuries, and thus ensured the unbroken transmission of the teachings despite the suppression of the monasteries. In the beginning of the eleventh century, a revitalizing stream of teachings began to appear in the form of 'treasures', deposited by Padmasambhava. From then on the Nyingma school was adorned and strengthened by the revelations of over 100 'tertons', 'treasure travellers', who not only discovered these treasures but practised and transmitted them to disciples.

The Sakya School

The Sakya School actually began in the year 1073, with the foundation of a meditation centre in the province of Tsang at a place called Sakya (grey earth). The centre was founded by a master called Konchog Gyalpo who hailed from the Khon' clan, an influential, aristocratic family whose connection with Buddhism went back to the time of Guru Padmasambhava in the eighth century. The members of this family had been practitioners of the 'ancient' tantras but in the mid-eleventh century Konchog Gyalpo and his brothers became convinced that many of the tantrik practices of the ancient transmission had been compromised by the dubious behaviour of some of their adherents. Therefore they looked to the new tantras that were being propagated in Tibet at that time. It was from

Konchog Gyalpo that the Sakya tradition really turned from being a small scale grouping into one of the greatest schools that the Buddhist world has ever seen. This transformation is due largely to the work of the Five Great Masters'. This eminent series of spiritual masters of the twelfth and thirteenth centuries were all members of the Khon family, which has remained to this day the ruling dynasty of the Sakya School. However, the fourth of these great masters, Kunga Nyingpo—usually known as Sakya Pandita—was the greatest of the early Sakya masters. He is famed as the only Tibetan master to possess the outer signs and characteristics of a fully enlightened Buddha. Sakya Pandita could be described as a 'Renaissance Man', combining as he did, spiritual accomplishment with an encyclopaedic knowledge of both Buddhist learning and the secular arts and sciences taught in India, such as poetics, lexicography, music, logic and epistemology. The Sakya Pandita introduced these disciplines to the Tibetan world, and for this he earned a reputation among all Tibetans as being the incarnation of the 'Manjushri', the bodhisattva of wisdom. Even during his lifetime Sakya Pandita's fame was so extensive that philosophers of the Hindu Vedanta School came from India to debate with him. He defeated each of them in turn through his mastery of logic and thus compelled them to convert to Buddhism.

The nephew of the Sakya Pandita, Chosgyal Phagpa (1235–1280), would ensure that more was to follow. He not only took up the mantle from Sakya Pandita of directing the Sakya School but became the lama of the world-famous Mongol Emperor – Kublai Khan, who had established control over the entire Chinese Empire. In return for his master's teachings, the

Khan established the Sakya School as rulers of Tibet, a position they held for the next 70 years. This was a time when the Sakya School stamped its genius upon Tibetan Buddhism.

Following the decline of its secular power, the Sakya School concentrated entirely upon spiritual matters, eventually giving rise to two great sub-sects—the Ngor, founded by Kunga Zangpo and Tshar, founded by Losal Gyamtso. Even in the nineteenth century the spiritual influence of the Sakya School was undiminished, playing as it did a major role in the ecumenical renaissance that took place in the Eastern Tibet.

The Kagyu School

While the Sakya School is marked for its eminence in scholarship and tantrik ritual, the Kagyu School is famed as the school of meditation and yogic practice. One of its alternative name is, 'the practice lineage'. Like the Sakya School, the Kagyu rose in the eleventh century at the time of renewed thirst in Tibet for authentic teaching. The founding patriarchs of the Kagyu School were Marpa, the translator, Milarepa, the great ascetic yogin and poet, and the incomparable Gampopa, monk, scholar and foremost systematizer of the Kagyu School.

Marpa (1012–1097) spent approximately 20 years in India over the course of three separate expeditions from Tibet. From renowned and accomplished masters such as Naropa and Maitripa, he inherited a body of teachings that would form the core spiritual syllabus for later generations of Kagyu practitioners in Tibet. Although Marpa was a translator, scholar and tantrik yogin, to all outward appearances he lived the life of a wealthy farmer, married to the lady Dagmema, and the father of several children. However, his close disciples recognized him as a Buddha in person. Marpa had intended to transmit his spiritual authority to his older son but this proved impossible and instead the lineage passed to his student, the poet and yogin, Milarepa. Milarepa (1052–1123) is famed throughout the Tibetan world, not just as a patriarch of the Kagyu, but as one of the paramount examples of the diligence and courage needed on the spiritual path. This great yogi of Tibet was born in a rich family, in the first autumn month, on the twenty-fifth day of AD 1052 under the influence of an auspicious star. His father gave him the name Thopaga ('delightful to hear'). His father died when he was seven. His uncle, who became incharge of his estate, mistreated Milerapa and his mother and Milarepa had to rise above a deluge of obstacles to become a student at the age of 38. In order to please his mother Milerapa learned black-magic and destroyed his enemies by launching a hailstorm. Later, however, he repented this very much and turned to the 'white path' or the path of virtue. Marpa was Milarepa's Guru, who made him pass through rigorous tests. With great difficulty, Milarepa got the highest initiation from his guru, and became his favourite disciple. Unlike his guru, who enjoyed marital bliss and bore children, Milerapa practised and lived in great austerity. He practised severe austerities and meditation in solitary caves and upon snowy mountains of Nepal and Tibet, clad only in a white cotton robe. He would sit shut up in a cave in a rigid posture, with a lamp over his head and meditated till the lamp was out. Food would be passed by Marpa's servant to him, through an aperture in the cave. Owing to such austerity, his body was reduced to a skeleton.

He followed the instructions of his guru and developed various *sidhis* or powers. He gained the power to take as many forms as he wished. Milarepa eventually attained Buddha-hood in his very lifetime through almost superhuman effort and went on to transmit his realization to his disciples. Milerapa has become an unceasing inspiration to countless generations of practitioners. The caves where he practiced devotion and meditation are even now places of pilgrimage and worship. He had a large number of followers. Even now there are people in Tibet who belong to his school. He died in AD 1135 at the age of 84.

The Gelug School

Like the Sakya and Kagyu Schools, the Gelug School too belongs to the group of the new tantra schools that were being established in the late fourteenth and early fifteenth centuries. By that time, the transmission of Buddhism from India to Tibet had long ceased and Buddhism was fully Tibetan. This situation is reflected in the fact that the school's founder, Tsong Khapa, did not have to travel to India but was rather able to inherit the teachings and practices for his new tradition from Tibetan masters of other schools.

In many ways Tsong Khapa was the synthesizer of the philosophical and meditative teachings of other schools. He wove together textual lineages and tantrik material from various traditions to provide the Gelug with its body of teachings. Most importantly he drew upon the approach of Atisa and the Kadam School. Tsong Khapa's innovation is visible in his philosophical teachings that attracted some criticism from other philosophers. Another important element in the Gelug curriculum was the study of logic and epistemology, to which Tsong Khapa gave more emphasis than had earlier Tibetan masters. Tsong Khapa was perhaps most notable for his insistence upon the strict observance of the rules of monastic disciple as put forth in the vinaya or monastic discpline, due to which his school was dubbed the Gelug (the virtuous way).

During Tsong Khapa's lifetime many disciples collected around him, so many that they were able to establish the monastery of Ganden, 35mi. from Lhasa. Shortly thereafter, two other monasteries, Sera and Drepung, were founded. Over the next two centuries, the school built up a very substantial membership and strong support throughout Tibet.

6
Reincarnation (Tracing the 'Tulkus')

SOMETIME DURING THE FOURTEENTH CENTURY a radical innovation occurred in Tibetan Buddhism—the appearance of the unprecedented concept of the reincarnation of a lama. This concept was to irrevocably change the body politic from a hierarchy to a theocracy in the ensuing time period. In Tibetan, 'incarnation' is 'sprul-sku' (Sanskrit: 'Nirmankaya') and better translated would be 'emanation body'. In contrast 'reincarnation' in Tibetan is 'yang-srid', it literally means 'again exist' and is used to identify an individual who is considered to be the 'rebirth' of an ancestor. Whereas the doctrine of 'incarnation' dates from the early days of the Mahayana form of Buddhism, the 'reincarnation' is unique as understood in Tibetan Buddhism.

Tibetans believe that all beings of various forms are reborn. In each life, the proportion of pain and joy which they experience is determined by their good or evil deeds in the previous life, known as the law of Karma. The idea embodied in the 'reincarnation' was derived from the basic Buddhist concept of rebirth. According to this concept the Buddhas or saints whose bodies are invisible to man, are reincarnated in the shape of priests of pious virtue for the salvation of the people. The scope of this reincarnation is rather comprehensive in Tibet, for almost every lama with any pretensions above the common level believes that he is destined to be reborn into the world for salvation. The Indians were never able to develop the spiritual technology whereby controlled rebirth could be achieved as a social institution. This did not occur until Buddhism was dispersed into Tibet and cross-fertilized with the great Himalayan mystics of Central Asia. These currents together produced the institution of the 'Tulku' or officially recognized reincarnate lama. This lama being considered a re-embodiment of a saintly ancestor's existence in a reincarnation of the same being in a new appearance, discovered anywhere in a child born at the right time and recognized by the leading monks and lamas. Tibet came to cherish the phenomenon as its greatest innovations, pouring a tremendous amount of its energy into the production of its reincarnate lamas. For the past eight centuries Tibet has produced a great many of these Tulkus. While the term 'Bodhisattva' and the Bodhisattva ideal is relatively well known, that of the 'Tulku' is much less so, for the 'Tulku' is a purely Tibetan conception that grew out of the idea of the Bodhisattva and it is of comparatively recent origin. The word 'Tulku' comes from two Tibetan words 'Tul' meaning 'Phantom' and 'Ku' meaning 'body', which implies that the person seen is not the real person, that his body is of the phenomenal and not of the 'real', a shell that is useful merely as an object of sense perception for other people. Hence his birth is not truly related to his family, a fact that is accepted and taken for granted by his family. The 'Tulku' better known as Incarnate Lama, is a Bodhisattva, but not all Bodhisattvas are Tulkus. Anyone born with a sufficient sense of dedication to take the Bodhisattva vow and if he is cognizant of it, is a Bodhisattva in the making. It may even be his first time, but he will be setting foot on the Bodhisattva path. On the other hand any reincarnating Bodhisattva may take this vow each time as a reaffirmation to himself and the world of his destiny. All 'Tulkus' also automatically take this vow unless they are prevented by external circumstances. So the taking of the vow in itself is no indication of the level of development attained.

The first time the concept of the 'Tulku' came into being was as late as AD 1474. The famous TsongKhapa, who reformed Tibetan Buddhism after it had fallen into disrepute and malpractices and who also founded the 'Yellow Hat Sect', had a disciple Ganden Trub-Pa who became his successor and founded the Tashi Lhrumpo Monastery, of which he became the head lama until he died in 1472. Two years after his death a baby boy, just learning to talk, began prattling about the life of this lama and of the monastery, where he had lived, although by no means could he have had any knowledge of it under normal circumstances. The parents therefore consulted the lamas of this monastery. The lamas, taking along with them an assortment of articles some of which had belonged to the late head lama, went to see the boy at his cottage. The little child seized only those articles which had belonged to Ganden Trub-Pa, the late head lama. This convinced the lamas that the little boy was the real reincarnation of Ganden Trub-Pa. From then on the hunt for the reincarnated head lama of every monastery was invariably made, it being assumed that they also were all reincarnated.

The ability to remember one's previous existence shows a higher order of development because it means one must have been completely self-conscious at the moment of one's death, and have retained a degree of this consciousness through the shock of delivery, which is comparable to the sudden awakening from sleep at which moment the dream vanishes and cannot be recalled. Yet not all 'Tulkus' remember this since they are at different levels of evolution, but the genuine 'Tulku', whether he remembers or not, is one who reincarnates for the sole purpose of benefiting mankind. He may be born in any part of the world but only in Tibet, Laddakh and Mongolia is he sought out and named a 'Tulku'.

Certain questions certainly arise about the concept of the 'Tulku' when it appears new and strange and is not taken for granted having been taught from childhood. For example, if the first 'Tulku' was identified as late as 1474, how are those identified who are said to date back much further, some even to the Buddha's own days?

The second question which inevitably arises concerns 'Tulkus' who do not appear to be much better than other men, who show a liking for the pleasures of the world and exhibit the weaknesses of the human nature. Some such leave the robes and marry and live worldly lives in money making and enjoyment. Others may show merely slight defects. There are three explanations offered for this:

The lamas admit that it is possible to make a mistake in the matter of identification and it is admitted that all 'Tulkus' are not true 'Tulkus'. It sometimes happens that the head of a monastery dies and no successor is found. He apparently has not reincarnated again, or at any rate not in the right quarter of the globe. If, as the years go by, the monastery shows signs of disintegrating through lack of a head, the senior lamas will inform the Dalai Lama and request him to identify the reincarnation for them. If he considers it necessary for the good of the monastery he will then do this and the rank and file and the laity as well, will believe him to be the true reincarnation of the head lama.

The second answer puts forward a hypothesis that is hard to comprehend; according to this hypothesis, if a 'Tulku' does evil deeds, he only apparently does them; it is due to the non-development of the witnesses that they think he is doing what he is not really doing at all. For, example, the conduct of the sixth Dalai Lama, who was a rake and a libertine of ill fame, profoundly shocked the Tibetans of his day. Yet they white-washed him with the excuse that he acted deliberately to test their faith, instead of admitting that he was a case of mistaken identity, which would have been far more probable.

Despite these discrepancies attached to the institution of the Tulku, the reverence and awe in which a 'Tulku' is held by the peasantry is incredible. They regard him more than a man and is even afraid to touch him because of his imagined divine qualities, stemming from the more rational belief that he is the vehicle for the oral transmission of esoteric knowledge, for the 'Tulku' is most highly trained.

The Dalai Lama has said about the somewhat incomprehensibleness of the institution of the 'Tulku' – 'many people might find the theory of reincarnation quite mysterious. In a way it is a bit complicated. But on the other hand, I feel that the Tibetan religious tradition of a high lama is quite democratic. The reincarnations of many high lamas have come from humble and ordinary backgrounds', and further, 'belief in rebirth engenders a universal love for all living beings and creatures, in the course of their numberless lives and our own, have been our beloved parents, children, brothers, sisters, friends. And the virtues our creed encourages are those which arise from this universal love – tolerance, forbearance, charity, kindness, compassion.'

From the time he enters the monastery, usually between his seventh and ninth year, the Tulku spends the best part of every single day, learning by heart from the sacred texts and their commentaries. When he has learned an enormous quantity—some books are 1,000 pages long and these he may assimilate by dozens—he is then taught to reason and connect what he has learned. To assist this, he takes part in those famous philosophical disputes which are a sport with the lamas. If he shows promise through quick-wittedness, he may go on to the esoteric monastery college for further training. By the time they are independent heads of their own monasteries, they have acquired tremendous amount of knowledge. The traditions involved in lama training are said to have been handed down by word of mouth from the time of the Buddha himself, and brought to Tibet by Padmasambhava and other great gurus from India.

The 'Tulku' system is an extension of the logic of the Buddhist understanding of Karma and rebirth and the Mahayana system of spiritual development. According to Buddhist doctrine, every sentient being is reborn over and over again in a beginning-less cycle, and so from this point of view every sentient being is a reincarnation. Most of us, however, are unaware of this, and a few people remember their past lives. The reason for this can be found in the process of death, in which the coarser levels of consciousness drop away, resulting in the eradication of the personality of one's past life. Sometimes, however, the process is incomplete, particularly if one's past life contained particularly powerful events that left deep imprints.

According to Tibetan Buddhism, however, through meditative training it is possible to gain access to deeply buried memories of past lives and become consciously aware of them. This ability is considered to be common among advanced mediators, people who have learned to access subtle levels of mind. Such people are said to be able to perceive events of their past lives. At higher levels of realization, it is thought that people can even develop the ability consciously to choose a rebirth, rather than simply being helplessly drawn into it. Advanced Bodhisattvas are able to determine the life situations that best enable them to work for the benefit for others, and they can consciously will themselves into these situations.

Tibetan Buddhism has developed elaborate systems for detecting and testing candidates in order to ensure that the person recognized as a 'Tulku' is actually the reincarnation of a previous teacher. The most rigorous of these tests are those used to find a new Dalai Lama. Since he is regarded as the greatest of all incarnate lamas and is the temporal and spiritual leader of Tibet, it is extremely important that the right person be found, and for this purpose various fool-proof methods have been devised. There are many degrees of 'Tulkus', from the great incarnations like the Dalai Lamas, the Panchen Lamas, and the Gyelwa Karmapas to minor incarnations who are associated with a particular area or with a monastery. The degree of care given to the testing procedure varies accordingly. For minor incarnations, the choice is sometimes made after a perfunctory search and often motivated by political considerations. For major incarnations, however, a great deal of care is taken to ensure the accuracy of the process.

Some lamas make the process of finding a successor relatively easy: the Gyelwa Karmapas for instance, traditionally write detailed instructions to their followers concerning where they will be reborn, often including such information as family name, of one or more parents, and time of birth. Their disciples open the letter at a prearranged time after the Karmapa's death, follow the master's instructions, and according to tradition the predictions are always correct.

Most lamas, however, do not make it so easy for their disciples. In the case of the Dalai Lamas, when one is about to die, he will commonly make general predictions about his rebirth, but these must be supplemented by further tests in order to ensure that the correct incarnation is traced. When the thirteenth Dalai Lama foresaw his death, for example, he predicted that he would take rebirth in the eastern part of Tibet. After his death in 1933, this prediction was corroborated by a number of unusual signs, all pointing towards the east.

The logic of the 'Tulku' system is based on these ideas: all sentient beings are constantly reincarnating; and some exceptionable beings are pursuing the path to enlightenment, motivated by compassion and constantly working for the benefit of the others. Since it is possible in principle to determine one's past births, it stands to reason that some beings will continually reincarnate themselves in a distinguishable lineage in a particular place for a particular group of people.

7
Institution of the Dalai Lama

By the thirteenth century, the cultural milieu in Tibet had become dominated by Buddhism, which had adopted many features of the indigenous Shamanic religion Bon. Moreover the period of anarchy that followed the assassination of the Lang Darma's due to his severe anti-religious actions, resulted in Tibet being divided into small principalities. This political anarchy prevailed for almost 400 years and was finally broken by the revival of Buddhism during the thirteenth century rather than by the emergence of another line of kings. Politically Tibet remained divided amongst petty rival chiefs, whose fortunes waxed and waned leading to increase in the political importance of the monasteries. The monasteries were fast accumulating wealth and land and for guarding themselves against raids in those lawless times, they were built like fortresses. They became a symbol of stability as well as places of refuge. While the older Samye monastery rose to a position of pre-eminence in both scholarly and spiritual endeavour, the younger Sakya, was first to achieve a truly political authority.

The pivotal point in Tibetan history at which the evolution of its body politic was turned in the direction of a theocracy, came when the Mongols intervened in Tibetan affairs in the thirteenth century. It was the policy of the Mongol emperor Chingez Khan and his followers to subjugate a foreign land by offering its ruler a choice between submission and annihilation. Continuance of submission and the payment of tribute to the Mongols were assured by taking members of the ruler's family as hostages. In addition, the Mongols preferred to administer subjugated territories through local ecclesiastics whenever possible.

When the Mongols first invaded Tibet, they found a politically fragmented land with no identifiable ruler to negotiate submission. Subsequently, Sakya Pandita (scholar), the learned hierarch of the 'Khon' ruling family of the Sakya sect, was summoned to submit Tibet. Two of his nephews were taken to the camp as hostages. Following the death of the Sakya Pandita, in AD 1251, the two nephews were taken to the camp of the prince Kublai Khan. The brilliant and talented Phagpa impressed Kublai Khan and he invited the former to the imperial court and appointed him the first imperial preceptor and gave him authority over the whole of Tibet.

Phagpa returned with a Mongol military escort to Sakya and began taking steps to establish a centralized government. A census was taken and central Tibet was divided into 13 myriarchies (administrative districts, each comprising of 10,000 families) for taxation and administrative purposes. In keeping with the subjugation policy of the Mongols, most of the 13 myriarchs appointed were hierarchs themselves or members of hierarchic families. Thus by the end of the thirteenth century, Tibet once again had a central government, albeit one imposed by a foreign power whose military troops enforced the hierocratic rule of the Sakya lama as a regent of the Mongol Khan.

As stability in the Sakya regency began to wane early in the fourteenth century due in part to the protracted sibling rivalry for ruling power among the numerous offspring of the then late Sakya lama, the Mongols began to lose interest in the welfare of the Sakya. Consequently, Sakya was overthrown in the middle of that century by the combined Tibetan forces.

Reincarnation was then engendered in the Tibetan matrix by the political need to affect a transition from a hierocratic form of government based on 'charisma of person' to an institutionalized one dependent on 'charisma of office'. The theoretical purpose for the origination of the concept of reincarnation in the fourteenth century however, could only become a political reality in the seventeenth century.

Not long after the concept of reincarnation surfaced in Tibetan Buddhism, another religious development began that was to have a long range impact on Tibetan political history; namely, the great reformation movement led by Tsong Khapa. Tsong Khapa's reformed order came to be known as the Yellow Hat sect and his followers were first called Galdanpa, after Galden (Ganden) monastery, established by Tsong Khapa, near Lhasa. Along with the Sera and Drepung monasteries, Ganden became the power base for the gelukpa and helped re-establish Lhasa as a centre of influence. Whoever became abbot at Ganden, following Tsong Khapa's footsteps, also became official head of the entire gelukpa order. Tsong Khapa's illustrious disciple Gedun Truppa, posthumously regarded as the first Dalai Lama not only filled that role but quite another as his lineage was to become the single most important within the Buddhist hierarchy of Tibet.

Following the course of the sixteenth century history, Tibet seemed to be headed towards a viable separation of church and state. Continuation of this separation of church and state could well have led to a radically different form of government in Tibet, but it came to naught due to the stratagem on the part of the Yellow-Hat sect. Facing unrelenting military and religious harassment from his adversaries, the hierarch of the Yellow-Hats, the third Dalai Lama, travelled to Mongolia, where it is said he converted the great Altan Khan. After the third hierarch died in Mongolia, his reincarnation was discovered to be none other than the great grandson of Altan Khan himself. The fourth Dalai Lama, a Mongol, and the only one in the entire lineage not ethnically a Tibetan, was brought to Lhasa and installed as the hierarch of the Yellow-Hat sect. Thereafter the Mongols became devoted followers of the Dalai Lamas and the military might of their cavalry was at their beck and call.

The successive Dalai Lamas received continuous co-operation from both, the state as well as the church and the single factor perhaps most responsible for this continuous co-operation was the Bodhisattva doctrine. In the beginning, the reincarnation concept in Tibet seemed primarily concerned with the identity of the human antecessor, rather than a superhuman emanatory. A further embellishment of the innovative idea of reincarnation emerged when the fifth Dalai Lama became temporal and spiritual head of Tibet. A 'treasure text' (gter-ma) revealed that the Dalai Lama was, in truth the incarnation (sprul-sku) of the patron Bodhisattva of Tibet, Avalokitesvara.

Once the symbiotic nature of his ontological being was revealed by the 'gter-ma text', the Dalai Lama became both incarnate and reincarnate; a phenomenal manifestation of a nominal reality. Following this revelation, the charisma of the 'office' of the Dalai Lama, subordinated his charisma of 'person', so much so that the 'office' continued to function as an impersonalized governmental institution in spite of the individual actions of the Dalai Lama. The Bodhisattva doctrine therefore helped transform the religious culture of Tibet from shamanism to Buddhism in the medieval period; it encouraged the development of the unique concept of reincarnation of a lama; and by means of the traditional Mahayana acceptance of the incarnation of a Bodhisattva, it moulded a symbiotic theocracy in which the 'office' of the Dalai Lama symbolized the inseparable unity of 'church and state'.

Lama Drom, a disciple of Atisa, is the most important of all the early incarnations from the point of view of Tibet's religious history, for it was the work of Lama Drom which led to the emergence of the 'Kadampa Order' (begun by Atisa). The Kadampa order influenced all other sects of Tibetan Buddhism and became the dominant religious force in Central Asia. It has remained as such till today. Spiritually it was the lineages coming through Lama Drom Tonpa that most profoundly set the stage for the character to be assumed by the Dalai Lamas. The first Dalai Lama came to be regarded as the reincarnation of Lama Drom, thus inheriting the mythology, which then followed the office of the Dalai Lama from that time onwards.

THE DALAI LAMA

The term 'Dalai' was a title conferred upon the Lama Sonam Gyatso, the third Dalai Lama, by the Tumet Mongol ruler. This was the beginning of a great tradition. Subsequently the two incarnate lamas that preceded Sonam Gyatso were counted as the first and the second Dalai Lamas.

The First Dalai Lama

Gedun Truppa (1391–1474) was recognized as the first Dalai Lama after the death of Sonam Gyatso and attained Buddhahood in his lifetime. He was born at Shabtad in Tsang province and took lessons from Tsong Khapa, the founder of the gelukpa sect. He later on founded the Tashilhunpo monastery and became its first abbot. He was also known as Panchen Gedun Truppa and his becoming the first Dalai Lama coming was indeed the turning point in the history of Tibet.

The Second Dalai Lama

Gedun Gyatso (1476–1542) was born at Tanag Segme in Tsang and was recognized as the reincarnation of Gedun Truppa. He studied in Tashi Umpo and later became the abbot of the same Monastery. He also became the chief abbot of Depung Monastery and since then he and his reincarnations, till the fifth Dalai Lama, were the residents of the Depung Monastery.

The Third Dalai Lama

Sonam Gyatso, born at Tohlung near Lhasa, was the third Dalai Lama (1543–1588). He was recognized as the reincarnation of Gedun Gyatso, studied at the Depung Monastery and took his final initiation from Sonam Drakpa. He was a brilliant scholar and teacher. On the second invitation from Altan Khan, the Tumet Mongol chieftain, he visited him and was welcomed in person at Chahar, the Mongolian outpost. Sonam Gyatso imparted Buddhist teachings to the Khan and in honour received many presents.

Altan Khan conferred on Sonam Gyatso the title 'Talai' (in Mongolian) meaning 'the embodiment of ocean of wisdom'. Talai somehow became Dalai in English. Significantly, this title came to be inherited by his succeeding reincarnations. Altan Khan also gave Sonam Gyatso a seal inscribed with Dorje Chang, meaning 'Holder of the Thunderbolt'. Altan Khan received from him the title 'Religious King, Brahma of Land'.

Sonam Gyatso established a diplomatic office at Tongkhor, also known as Lusar, for maintaining close relationship with the Khan. He also founded the Lifthang Monastery in the Kham region. Altan Khan's son and successor, Dhuring Khan, invited Sonam Gyatso and on the way the Dalai Lama built a monastery of Kumbum, where his son Tsong Khapa was born.

The Fourth Dalai Lama and the Birth of the Institution of Panchen Lama

A child of a Mongolian tribal chief was recognized as the next Dalai Lama, the incarnation of Sonam Gyatso. He became the fourth Dalai Lama (1589–1616) with the title 'Yonten Gyatso'. He was given religious training by a Mongolian teacher.

At Depung Monastery he came into contact with a scholarly Lama, Lozang Chosgyan of Tashilhunpo, and studied under him. Lozang Chosgyan was recognized as the first Panchen Lama (meaning 'Great Scholar') and thereafter his reincarnations inherited this title.

In 1615 the Shen-tsung, Emperor of China, beseeched the fourth Dalai Lama to bless the Buddhist temple in Nanking.

Because of heavy commitments, the Dalai Lama could not go there but blessed it from Tibet itself.

The Fifth Dalai Lama

The fifth Dalai Lama was recognized in the person of Ngwang Lozong Gyatso (1617–1682). He was ordained by the Panchen Lama in 1625. In 1638, Gushri Khan, the chief of the Qoshot Mongols, received religious instructions from the fifth Dalai Lama who was given the title 'Tenzin Choskyi Gyalpo' (Religious King and Holder of the Buddhist faith). The Dalai Lama sent a permanent representative to Mongolia for maintaining good relations. In Tibet, however, things were difficult as there was a rivalry in the ruling circle. In the climax of rivalry between the Tsangpa Depa and Kyisod Depa, the latter sought help from Gushri Khan who first defeated the Beri chieftain in the east, and eventually crushed the power of Tsangpa Depa. Having conquered most part of Tibet in 1642, he requested the fifth Dalai Lama to rule the country. Thus, Tibet once again became united under a single legitimate government.

The fifth Dalai Lama was an effective ruler and good administrator besides being an excellent diplomat. He built palaces and monasteries and during his time peace prevailed in the state. The Dalai Lama also visited Peking on the repeated invitation of the Manchu Emperor of China. The emperor presented a gold plate to the Dalai Lama inscribed with the title 'Dalai Lama Dorje Chang' meaning 'Superior, the ocean, Holder of the Thunderbolt' in Manchu, Tibetan and Chinese scripts. The emperor in turn received a gold plate inscribed with a legend 'Namgyi Lha Jamyang Gongma Dakpa Chenpo' (The

Great Master, Superior one, God of the sky, Bodhisattva). The Dalai Lama returned to Lhasa in 1653.

Three years after the demise of Panchen Lozang Chosgyan, (the first Panchen Lama) at the age of 91 in 1662, a three-year-old boy was observed to be the reincarnation of the Panchen Lama and was recognized so by the Dalai Lama. He was given the name 'Lozang Yeshe' and taken to Tashilhunpo monastery. In his last days the Dalai Lama appointed Sangye Gyatso as Desi (regent), in 1679. In 1682, the fifth Dalai Lama expired in the Potala. History bears it out that in his personality were combined the rare qualities of a great statesman and an outstanding scholar.

Sangye Gyatso, the Desi or regent, is accused of concealing the demise of the fifth Dalai Lama for thirteen long years. He in fact was able to carry on the deception well. However, when the Potala Palace was completed in 1695, he unhesitatingly announced the death of the Dalai Lama.

The Sixth Dalai Lama

The sixth Dalai Lama, Tsangyang Gyatso (1683–1707), was born at Mon Tawang. The Panchen Lama administered the initial vows. The sixth Dalai Lama, however, did not abide by the monastic rules and he was neither interested in the affairs of the state nor in performing the Dalai Lama's obligations. He in fact enjoyed the company of women, and also composed excellent romantic verses and songs. Understandably, he was soon deposed from his exalted position.

The government of Tibet, popularly known as 'Ganden Phodrang', had consolidated its power under the dynamic leadership of the fifth Dalai Lama and the wise administration of successive Desis or regents, specially the Desi Sangye Gyatso. Gushri Khan the Mongol Chief remained in Tibet to assist the Dalai Lama and advise the Desi in his work of efficient governance. After the declaration of fifth Dalai Lama's death, Lhasang Khan, a descendant of Gushri Khan, somehow developed differences with Desi Sangye Gyatso. Lhasang Khan had become ambitious of himself becoming the Desi and therefore disputed the authenticity of the Tsangyang Gyatso as the real reincarnation of the fifth Dalai Lama. He even installed another person, named Yeshi Gyatso, as the sixth Dalai Lama. But the monasteries and the people of Tibet did not recognize him as the reincarnation of the Dalai Lama. In this uncertain situation the force of Lhasang Khan managed in 1707 to take Tsangyang Gyatso to Mongolia. It is said that on the way itself he had passed away.

Lhasang Khan ruled Tibet till 1717. But the fact of the matter is that Tibet was not under the Mongolian rule but a Mongolian person had become the head of Tibetan government. The government was in continuity with the legitimate government set up by the fifth Dalai Lama in 1642.

Another Mongolian Jungar chief, named Tse Wang Rabten, who had enemity with the tribe to which Lhasang Khan belonged, attacked Tibet, killed Lhasang Khan in 1717 and thus took the power to rule Tibet.

The Seventh Dalai Lama

The seventh Dalai Lama, Kalsang Gyatso (1708–1757), was born at Lithang in Kham province. The infant boy was recognized as the seventh Dalai Lama and was given protection by some Mongolian tribes and taken to Koko Nor region. He was warmly received by the Mongols. The Mongols and Manchu Emperor sent a garrison of military for his protection and brought him to Lhasa with force. On receiving the information of the Seventh Dalai Lama coming with large military force of Manchu and Mongols, the Jungars chose to flee from Lhasa and returned to Jungar region in Mongolia. After the successful installation of Dalai Lama in Potala Palace in Lhasa a seven member committee was set up temporarily to fill up the power vacuum created by the sudden departure of Jungars. The seven member committee included two Mongolians, two Manchus and three Tibetans. This was done by the Tibetan officials after the departure of Jungars but in consultation with the leaders and military commanders who had accompanied the seventh Dalai Lama. The Mongolian troops were withdrawn immediately but the Chinese garrison remained in Lhasa in the pretext of peace-keeping. After one year, the temporary committee was dissolved and the power was handed over to the council of ministers under the seventh Dalai Lama. This council of ministers consisted of Ngapho, Lumpa and Jarawa from U, and Sonam Gyalpo and Sonam Topgyal from Tsang.

The Eighteenth and the Nineteenth Centuries: Struggle for Power

Unfortunately, soon thereafter arose sharp differences among the council of ministers in Tibet. In the unsettled conditions, the provincial matter gained prime interest among the council of ministers. Then one day, during the absence of Pholha, the most important minister, the other three ministers conspired and killed one of the ministers, Sonam Gyalpo, which led to a civil war in 1727 in which the leading players were Pholha on the one side and the remaining ministers on the other side. Pholha sought military support from China. China under the Manchus gladly took it as the golden chance to send its military to intervene in Tibet's internal affairs. The strong Chinese military force was placed under the command of Jalangga and Mailu (an Amban) for effective intervention but before the Chinese reached the capital, Pholha had won the war and taken full control of Lhasa. Still, the fact remains that he did not prevent the Manchu army from reaching Lhasa in 1728. They forced Pholha to give concessions and post two Manchu officials (Ambans) in Tibet with garrison of armies in the pretext of their security and to guard Tibet from possible invasion of Jungars. These officials were supposed to act as liaison between the Tibetan rulers and the Manchu Emperor in China although in effect by promptly sending information about Tibetan affairs they helped China in controlling Tibet, indirectly.

The Council of Ministers was reorganized with Pholha wielding the real power. He was an efficient administrator and ensured that the monasteries were well maintained.

Pholha established a permanent military force with 3,000 armed personnel and then asked the Manchu Emperor to withdraw the Chinese garrison as the Tibetans were now capable of defending themselves from any foreign invasion. He succeeded in reducing the Chinese force to only 100 armies, but the Ambans at Lhasa continued to play a mischievous role in creating divisions and mistrust among the Tibetan high officials in order to weaken the Tibetan government and make it dependent on the Chinese support and supervision. The, Pholka's brother Tsetan Namgyal was misled by the Ambans and this resulted in a bitter fight between the brothers. Due to this, the Pholha lost faith in many of his ministers who were under the influence of the cunning Ambans. Realising all these misdeeds, he finally gave an ultimatum to the Chinese to call back the remaining 100 armed forces within a specified time failing which they would have to face severe consequences. Unfortunately, due to aggressiveness and apparent arrogance he was not very popular among his own officials. At this point, the Ambans invited him to their office to receive an important communication from the Manchu Emperor, and there he was treacherously killed in 1750. Immediately, a few of his trusted aids retaliated and killed both the Ambans and many other Chinese stationed along with them. The Dalai Lama rose to the occasion and restored peace and order. The senior minister Doring Pandita was then asked to carry on the administration and again taking advantage of the situation Chinese Emperor there upon sent a strong military contingent.

Stress and strains continue between the Tibetans and the Chinese, in which the Dalai Lama emerges Supreme. Pholha was succeeded by his younger son Gyumey Namgyal, who disliked the Chinese presence. Outwardly he showed that he was friendly with the Ambans, but in effect he persuaded the Chinese Emperor to reduce the strength of the Chinese garrison in Tibet. The Dalai Lama assumed more powers as the chief executive and head of the government. Due to which his temporal authority was established on a permanent basis and was never challenged afterwards. The seventh Dalai Lama died in 1757 after consolidating the authority of the politico-religious institution he headed.

The Eighth to Twelfth Dalai Lama—A Quick Succession

The eighth Dalai Lama, Jampal Gyatso (1758–1804) was the only one who lived a comparatively long life. Unfortunately, it was during the times of this Dalai Lama that war with the Gorkhas broke out during 1788–92. But all through his life the Dalai Lama was immersed in religious matters and did not like political administration which he left conveniently in the hands of the regents.

Before the Gorkha advance in Nepal in 1769, the Mallas were the rulers of the country. The Mallas had strong Buddhist leanings and were friendly with Tibet and carried on trade and currency transactions. The Gorkhas were by and large very aggressive. Soon border disputes and trade and monetary troubles cropped up. They sent an army in 1788 and occupied several border districts of Tibet. However, they withdrew on being promised a tribute. The Dalai Lama had no hand in this agreement. After one single instalment of the tribute, the Dalai Lama stopped it. This was, however, taken to be a violation of the treaty which resulted in an invasion by the Gorkhas. During this invasion the second invasion by the Gorkhas reached upto Shingatse in 1792; it ravaged the Tashilhunpo Monastery.

During the first attack of the Gorkhas, the Tibetan Government sought the Chinese military support. The Chinese sent a small number of troops but they refused to fight against the Gorkhas and persuaded the Tibetan authorities to agree to the terms of the Gorkhas against their wishes. On the second attack, in 1792, however, the Chinese reinforced their troops and joined the Tibetan army which pushed back the Gorkhas upto Kathmandu. At that time a treaty was concluded between

Nepal and Tibet in the presence of the Chinese representatives. In that treaty the Chinese very cunningly managed to force both Tibet and Nepal to accept their protectorate.

The Chinese military took advantage of their presence in Lhasa during this period and started interfering in the internal administration of Tibet. They prepared a document, the so-called 'Guidelines for the Administration', consisting of 29 points. In this they tried to show that the Chinese had control over Tibet since it projected the Ambans equal to the Dalai Lama with the authority to take part in the decision-making process of Tibetan affairs. It also made certain provisions for making appointments of the high-level officials by the Chinese emperor. Obviously, it was not favoured but due to adverse circumstances prevailing at that time the Tibetans could not force its withdrawal, even though it was never implemented in letter and spirit.

After the demise of the eighth Dalai Lama in 1804 there appeared on the scene two claimants for the ninth Dalai Lamaship, one from Kham and the other from Amdo region; both the boys were two years old.

They were brought before the Regent, and the Kashag (Tibetan Parliament) at Lhasa. They found the boy from Dan Chokhar, in Kham, successful in the test, and chose him to be the ninth Dalai Lama with the name 'Lungtok Gyustso' (1806–1815). When he was ten years old he took part in the annual Monlam festival and in the cold he unfortunately developed pneumonia and died.

During that time Chinese power waned and the monks from China, living in Tibet, persuaded the monks of the three important and large monasteries—Depung, Sera and

Ganden—to prevail upon the Government to ban the entry of foreigners into Tibet. The government accepted this and issued orders to the border district officers to prevent foreigners from coming into Tibet. This was, however, a retrograde step which isolated Tibet from the outside world affecting the progress of the country which other nations achieved. Because of this, knowledge about Tibet was denied to outsiders and vice versa.

For the tenth Dalai Lama, Ishultrem Gyatsol, two claimants appeared from U-Tsang and three from Kham. At the end, the Lithang child was chosen as he satisfied the Regent's and Kashag's tests. Unfortunately, the Dalai Lama suffered ill-health throughout and died in 1837.

The eleventh and twelfth Dalai Lamas, Khedrup Gyatso (1838–1856) and Trinle Gyatso (1856–1875) also expired within a couple of decades after their enthronement. The thirteenth Dalai Lama Tupden Gyatso (1876–1933), proved to live much longer, and he became one of the greatest rulers in Tibetan history. After the death of the twelfth Dalai Lama Trinle Gyatso, the search parties began looking for his reincarnation in southeast Tibet, as this location had been revealed in a vision at Hlamo Latso, a lake located about 90mi. southeast of Lhasa.

The Thirteenth Dalai Lama

The thirteenth Dalai Lama was born in 1876 in Takpo Langdun in southeast Tibet and recognized in 1878 as the reincarnation of Trinle Gyatso. Tupden Gyatso was born into a peasant family, and he was enthroned as Dalai Lama during a time of increasing tension for Tibet. He ascended to full power in 1895 and began a programme to modernize the country. Some of his public statements indicate that he recognized Tibet's lack of friends in the international community and the danger posed by the winds of change brewing in China, which would eventually engulf his country. And China was not the only external danger as was made clear in 1903, when a British expedition led by Col. Francis Younghusband entered Tibet and demanded that the government open trade relations with British India.

Younghusband's troops marched into Lhasa and forced the Tibetan government to agree to a trade pact that was highly favourable to Britain. His mission accomplished, Younghusband withdrew from Tibet, but in 1909 a new threat emerged on its borders. The ease with which Younghusband's troops had entered Tibet clearly showed how militarily weak the country was at that time, and the Chinese general Chao Erh-feng decided to capitalize on the situation by staging a series of raids into the territory claimed by the Tibetan central government. Chao intended to end the period of merely nominal Chinese rule of Tibet and annex the country. In 1910, Chao easily reached Lhasa, but the Dalai Lama had fled to India, along with his ministers, and so there was no one with whom he could negotiate surrender. Chao's advance to Lhasa had been accompanied by widespread brutality, and a number of monasteries had been sacked. Many Tibetans had been tortured or killed. Thus general came to be known among Tibetans as 'Chao the butcher'.

In 1907 he sent military expedition into Kham, which seized thousands of loads of grain from the local inhabitants without making any repayment. The Throne Holder of Ganden and Kashag (Tibetan Parliament) sent a letter to protest to the Amban Lien-yu, but he refused to forward it to Beijing.

Although this was interpreted by the Tibetans as a sign that the Ambans were in collaboration with Chao, it was probably a reflection of the emperor's weakness as well. As the Manchu dynasty was breaking up, some of its generals were acting independently of the central government and pursuing their own programmes of conquest and pillage.

Chao's forces attempted to usurp control of Tibet but were met with widespread resistance by the Tibetan people, who refused to cooperate with the invaders. In order to consolidate his power, he publicly announced that the Dalai Lama, who was still in India, was being removed from office. The proclamation, however, was widely ignored by the Tibetans, who continued to wait for his return. In 1911 the nationalists overthrew the Manchu dynasty. When the news reached Lhasa, some of the Chinese troops mutinied, and Chao retreated to his capital in Szechuan. He was executed in 1912 by the nationalist leader Yin Ch'iang-heng. The dispirited Chinese troops left behind in Tibet eventually (Tibetan Parliament) surrendered. When Tibetan control was restored, the Kashag, realizing that there was no longer any need for the Chinese overlordship or the remnants of the 'priest–patron' relationship and expelled all Chinese officials and soldiers.

Soon after gaining control over China, the nationalists began to set their sights on Tibet, which they recognized as having strategic importance due to its location at the top of Central Asia, having borders with India, Nepal, Mongolia and Russia. Another consideration was a Chinese belief that Tibet contained vast stores of natural resources, which was reflected in the Chinese term for the region: 'Xizang', meaning 'Western Treasure House'. The new government soon began asserting a hereditary right to Tibet, claiming that it had been a Chinese vassal since the twelfth century. The Tibetan government quickly realized the threat posed by a resurgent China and moved to sever all relations. There was no longer any possibility of renewing the 'priest–patron' relationship, since the nationalists were absolutely secular. With China now threatening to annex Tibet and assume effective control, Tibet formally declared its independence.

Despite its inability to influence Tibet's internal affairs, the Chinese nationalist government continued to proclaim its sovereignty over the country. For the next several decades China was in a state of internal turmoil, which eventually ended with the defeat of the nationalists by the communists led by Mao Zedong. The interregnum period allowed Tibet a brief respite, but this proved to be merely the calm before a growing storm.

After his return to Lhasa, the Dalai Lama, recognizing Tibet's tenuous position in relation to its neighbours, initiated several measures designed to protect the country and bring it into the international community. He began by creating Tibet's first standing army, which was financed by a tax on all estates in Tibet. This led to a conflict with the Panchen Lama, whose monastery of Tashilunpo was the most powerful landowning institution in the country. The Panchen Lama lost the confrontation and was forced to flee to China in 1923.

In order to foster an understanding of the outside world, the Dalai Lama sent a number of young Tibetans to England for schooling, and he also attempted to create a western style system of education in Tibet. This move was strongly resisted by the monastic leadership, who saw it as a threat to their long-standing hegemony over education and who feared that foreign ideas might undermine the position of Buddhism in Tibet. The monasteries had become deeply conservative and resistant to change, and their leaders were strongly opposed to any innovations in society or religion. Despite the nominal supremacy of the Dalai Lama, their power was so great that their conservatism eventually defeated his attempt at modernizing the educational system.

With the death of the thirteenth Dalai Lama in 1933, Tibet again entered into an interregnum period. This occurred at an inopportune time, because a combination of Chinese manipulation of foreign powers and Tibetan insularity had isolated the country from the outside world. In his attempts to enlist foreign allies, the thirteenth Dalai Lama discovered that Tibet had no friends in the international community and utterly lacked the military resources to repel a determined foreign invasion. On its borders a new power was growing, one that would eventually engulf Tibet, and all of the Dalai Lama's efforts to forestall catastrophy ultimately came to nothing. In a famous statement, shortly before his death, he warned his people of imminent danger from foreign invasion and predicted that unless Tibet adopted his modernization policies the country would be overrun, its people killed or enslaved and its religion destroyed. Despite his personal authority, however, after his death his reforms were mostly scuttled and Tibet returned to its policy of deeply conservative isolationism.

In January 1934, Reting Rinpoche Jambel Yeshe was selected to be the regent during the interregnum period. The monastic leaders in Lhasa insisted that the regent can be an incarnate lama (sprul sku). When the leading candidates withdrew their names from consideration, the choice fell to Reting Rinpoche, who at the time was only 24 years old. Although he was a widely respected tulku, he had little experience in the role of political leadership.

Unfortunately for the stability of the country, he proved to be corrupt and heavy handed in his rule. Although at the beginning of his reign his authority was limited, within a few years he gained supreme power in Tibetan politics. After consolidating his position, Reting Rinpoche began to openly flout the conventions of monastic behaviour, and his personal letters indicate that despite being a monk he engaged in affairs with women. There was also widespread speculation that he had sexual relations with men. In addition, he is reported to have spent money lavishly and recklessly.

The claimant for the fourteenth Dalai Lama was a very little boy of slightly more than two years, called Hlama Dondrup. Hlama Dondrup had to undergo a rigorous test before his claim could be accepted as genuine. He was first presented with a choice of prayer beads, and he chose the beads belonging to the thirteenth Dalai Lama without hesitation. Kutsang Rinpoche then presented him with two walking sticks. The boy at first reached for the wrong one but corrected himself later. This apparent mistake was actually seen as being very significant, since the first stick had briefly belonged to the thirteenth Dalai Lama before he gave it to a friend. The final choice was between the hand drum of the thirteenth Dalai Lama, which was rather worn out, and a beautifully crafted hand drum. Hlama Dondrup unhesitatingly chose the thirteenth Dalai Lama's drum and twirled it correctly too.

This test was significant but not definitive. Tradition holds that Dalai Lamas are marked with specific signs, and the boy was examined for these. Some of the signs are: large ears, long eyes, streaks on the legs, like a tiger's stripes, and a conch shell shaped imprint on one hand. All these were found on the boy, and this finally convinced the members of the search party that the correct incarnation had been located. The testing did not end there however. Given the importance of the Dalai Lama, it is necessary to be absolutely certain, and so after the authorities in Lhasa were notified of the search party's findings, the state oracles were consulted, and they confirmed that Hlama Dondrup was indeed the reincarnation of the thirteenth Dalai Lama.

The members of the search party also recognized that the area in which Hlama Dondrup was born, matched Reting Rinpoche's vision of the Tibetan letters a, ka, and ma in Hlama Latso. A is the first letter of Amdo, the province in which the village of Taktse is located, and ka is the first letter in Kumbum, the most important monastery of the area. In addition, ka and ma are a part of the name of monastery in Taktse, named Karma Shartsong.

The birth of the fourteenth Dalai Lama was accompanied by a number of auspicious signs. He was born at dawn on July 6, 1935, and when he emerged from his mother's womb, his eyes were wide open, which she thought was very unusual. As soon as he was born, his father recovered from his illness. Also shortly after his birth, two crows (who are associated with the Buddha Mahakala) sat on the roof of the house for a while, a similar event had occurred with the births of the first, seventh, eighth and twelfth Dalai Lamas. As he grew, his parents realized that he was unusually bright.

Although the search party was eager to bring the young Dalai Lama to Lhasa, their departure was prevented by the intervention of a Muslim warlord named Ma Bufeng, whose troops controlled the area. Aware of the Dalai Lama's importance to the Tibetans, Ma Bufeng exploited the situation by demanding a sum of $92,000 in exchange for his permission to take the child away. When the Tibetans produced the amount, but he raised the price by $3,000,000 in addition to demanding valuable gifts, including the robes of the past Dalai Lama and an edition of the Buddhist canon. The Tibetans encountered great impediments in fulfilling the outrageous demands of the warlord but since the Dalai Lama was no less than god for them, they went to all lengths to raise the ransom and take the child to Lhasa.

On the morning of 6 October 1939, the search party arrived with the four year old, Dalai Lama to-be, at Lhasa. A huge tent encampment had been constructed on a plain about 2mi. from the city, in accordance with traditional protocol for the greeting of newly recognized Dalai Lamas. Prominent lamas and government officials gathered there, along with huge crowds of onlookers, and traditional ceremonies were performed. Two days later, on 8 October the Dalai Lama was escorted into the city, while a Tibetan band played 'God Save the King', learned by them from the British emissaries. Huge crowds turned out to witness the grandeur of the procession, and ambassadors from Nepal, India, China and Bhutan too were present. The Nechung oracle also attended, taking possession of the body of his human host and performing a dance in honour of the

Dalai Lama. Approaching the boy, the oracle bowed down and presented him with a ceremonial scarf, called a 'kata'. The young Dalai Lama placed it over the oracle's neck in blessing.

From there, the procession travelled to Norbulingka, summer residence of the Dalai Lamas. At Norbulingka a small incident fuither marked the authenticity of the 14th Dalai Lama Hlama Dondrup pointed at a small box and said, 'my teeth are in that box' and when the box was opened, it was discovered that it contained a set of dentures of the thirteenth Dalai Lama.

After several weeks, Hlama Dondrup was ordained as a Buddhist monk and given the ordination name of Jetsun Jambel Ngawang Losang Yeshe Tenzin Gyatso—most venerable, elegant glory, eloquent, intelligent, upholder of the teaching, ocean of wisdom. On February 22, 1940, shortly before his fifth birthday, Tenzin Gyatso was enthroned as the fourteenth Dalai Lama in a grand ceremony in the Potala palace. His official enthronement in 1940 was attended by representatives from the British government in India, the King of Nepal, the Maharajas of Sikkim and Bhutan, and a Chinese representative named Wu Chung-hsin.

During this period, the rest of the world was in the throes of World War II, but Tibet remained virtually untouched by the international conflict. An attempt to involve Tibet occurred in 1942, when the Chinese and British governments requested permission to build a supply route through Tibet because the route between India and China through Burma had been cut off by the Japanese. Unwilling to allow Chinese troops or supplies into its territory, Tibet refused the request. The Chinese government threatened to attack Tibet unless the government changed its position, but when Tibetan troops were sent to the border, the Chinese relented and withdrew the surveyors who had been sent to plan the road ahead.

After the conclusion of World War II, the Chinese communists made a bid for power, and soon after assuming full power the communist government made it clear that it intended to annex Tibet and make it a part of China. Deeply concerned about the obvious threat posed by the communists, in July 1949, the Tibetan government expelled all Chinese officials from the country.

On October, 1949, a new government that referred itself as 'The People's Republic of China' was inaugurated in Beijing. Now that China was united under a strong central government, it possessed much more power than the weak nationalists. The communists then announced that it intended to unite all of China and 'reintegrate' Tibet into the 'motherland'. Apparently believing that Tibet had always been a part of China, the communist leaders suspected that the expulsion of Chinese officials and the severance of relations had been due to interference by 'western imperialists' and 'counter revolutionaries'.

On 1 January 1950, the New Year broadcast from Beijing announced that in the coming year, the People's Liberation Army would liberate Tibet from foreign imperialists and reintegrate it with the motherland. In August of the same year, a massive earthquake shook Tibet, and its tremors were felt all over the country. The sky over Southeastern Tibet glowed with an ominous red glow, and people remembered that several years earlier the Nechung Oracle had faced eastward while in a trance and predicted a great agitation that would threaten

Tibet with danger. This had been followed by the appearance in 1949 of a bright comet in the sky, which was interpreted as a further harbinger of war. In addition, the top of an ancient column, at the base of the Potala, was found shattered one morning. This had been built in AD 763 in commemoration of Tibet's victory over China.

Following these events, reports came into Lhasa from the east indicating that Chinese troops were massing at the border. The Tibetans prepared to meet them with small, poorly armed, undisciplined local militias. The Chinese army was spearheaded by an advance force of 20,000 combat-hardened troops, armed with modern weapons. They were backed up by the world's largest army, consisting of 5 million soldiers – close to the total population of Tibet! When Chinese troops began pouring into Kham, the Tibetan militias were quickly and easily overcome. Kham was given up after only token resistance. With a foothold established in eastern Tibet, the People's Liberation Army set its sight on Lhasa.

Tenzin Gyatso's early years were mainly taken up with the intensive programme of study expected of Dalai Lamas, and during this time Tibet continued to be ruled by regents. With the Chinese incursions in eastern Tibet, the central government convened a special session with the two main state oracles, Nechung and Gadong. The Dalai Lama was in attendance, along with leading government officials and abbots from the leading monasteries. Both oracles indicated that he should assume power immediately, although he had not yet reached the normal age at which the Dalai Lamas take on their temporal duties. Taktra Rinpoche, who had succeeded Reting Rinpoche as a regent, resigned soon after, and the Dalai Lama assumed full temporal and religious control on 17 November 1950, at the age of 16.

The full extent of Tibet's friendliness in the international community was brought home when it appealed to the United Nations for help soon after the Dalai Lama's ascension to power. The members of the UN unwilling to provoke a conflict with China over a small and isolated country, rebuffed the Tibetans, stating that Tibet was not a member nation, and so its appeal would not be considered.

During the Dalai Lama's early tenure as a ruler, China made increasingly bold forays into eastern Tibet, meeting little effective resistance. The Dalai Lama attempted to come to terms with the Chinese government and to find a way to reach a peaceful agreement, but the Chinese leadership was bent on conquest.

After establishing a power base in eastern Tibet, the People's Liberation Army began moving to Lhasa. Along the way it met with sporadic but ineffectual Tibetan resistance, and on 9 September 1951, three thousand troops of the eighteenth Route Army marched into Lhasa, waving portraits of Mao Zedong and Zhou Enlai above their heads, holding aloft a Chinese flag with four small circles around a blazing yellow sun. The orbs symbolized the small states that China considered to be a part of its territory, and the sun was the Han—controlled central areas of China. One of the orbs was Tibet, which was now under direct Chinese control for the first time in its history.

Within months additional Chinese troops flooded into Lhasa. They were met by angry Tibetans, who shouted insults and spat at them. 20,000 Chinese troops initially exercised restraint, proclaiming that their invasion was a 'liberation' that would bring prosperity to Tibet, the Chinese promised schools, hospitals, roads and other modern improvements. The new overlords of Tibet soon constructed a theatre, bank and hospital, but ironically they were reserved for Chinese officials and Tibetan collaborators, while the masses were not permitted to sample these symbols of modernization.

It soon became clear that the foreign invaders and their ideology were incompatible with Tibetan culture. While the communists firmly believed that Marxism is the cure for all the world's problems and that communization would create a perfect society, the Tibetans looked for rewards beyond the present life, since as Buddhists they believed that any sort of mundane existence is unsatisfactory.

In spite of these differences, the Dalai Lama took on the task of negotiating with the Chinese. In July 1954, he accepted the invitation to meet with Mao in Beijing, hoping to forestall further Chinese aggression. Although he reported that his talks with the Chinese leader were cordial, when he returned to Tibet he saw that the invaders were in the process of transforming his homeland. By 1955 the process of collectivism was underway, with Kham and Amdo bearing the brunt of the changes at first. Chinese troops began confiscating arms, property and other possessions, and they also created communes. Local leaders, wealthy landowners and religious figures were rounded and subjected to public thamzing (struggle sessions), in which they were berated for their 'crimes against the people' and forced to confess. Confession was generally preceded by beating and often followed by execution. Local people who refused to participate were accused of being 'collaborators' or 'reactionaries'. Chinese soldiers commonly tortured monks and nuns in front of crowds of horrified Tibetans. Monks and nuns were made to forcibly copulate publicly and if they refused to do so, others were tortured until they complied. In order to break down resistance thousands of people were executed as 'counter-revolutionaries' and their families were then made to pay for the bullets used for killing them. These measures naturally led to rebellion, particularly in Kham and Amdo where bands of guerillas were formed. Some of their attacks on the Chinese were successful but their final defeat was inevitable.

By 1959 the situation in Tibet was grim. The country suffered under the yoke of a foreign army that was wrecking havoc throughout the country. As tensions increased, a message was delivered to the Dalai Lama by the Chinese general Dan Guansan, who was in command of the Chinese forces, to join him at a theatrical performance. The message stipulated that the Dalai Lama was to come alone, with no attendants or body guards.

Fearing that the invitation was part of a thinly disguised plot to kidnap Tibet's spiritual leader, the Dalai Lama and his advisors began planning his escape. When radio Beijing announced that he would attend the performance, the people of Lhasa, also suspecting a plan to kidnap him, took to the streets en masse in protest. At dawn, on 10 March 1959, a huge crowd of Tibetans gathered outside the Dalai Lama's summer palace, the Norbulingka, to prevent his capture by the Chinese. By 9 o'clock there were 30,000 people massed outside the gates, shouting anti-Chinese slogans. During the next several days tensions continued to mount, and it became clear that the Chinese leaders intended to take drastic action. At 4 o'clock on March 17th, the Chinese began lobbing mortar shells in the area around the Norbulingka, with the stated purpose of 'freeing' the Dalai Lama from the 'reactionary clique' surrounding his residence. Realizing that there was no point in continued negotiations with the Chinese, the Dalai Lama and his advisors made plans to leave that night. He and his family disguised themselves in order to pass by the Chinese patrols that roamed the countryside. The Dalai Lama dressed up as a soldier, taking off his glasses in order to make recognition more difficult.

Late that night, he slipped out of the Norbulingka, undetected, with his party and began the long journey of exile into India. On 28 March Zhou Enlai announced in a radio broadcast that the Tibetan government had been dissolved and China had taken direct control. After hearing the news, the Dalai Lama crossed the border into India to begin a new life in exile.

In the aftermath of the Dalai Lama's flight, the Chinese army went on an orgy of destruction. As thousands of corpses lay outside the Norbulingka, Chinese troops attacked Lhasa, shelling the Potala, destroying the medical college on Chokpori Hill, and bombing Ganden monastery into rubble. Tibet's second holiest shrine, the Rampoche temple, with thousands of people inside it, vainly hoping that the Chinese would not attack a temple, was set on fire and machine gunners opened fire as well at the same time, killing scores of people. Within days, the conquest of Tibet was complete, thousands of people lay dead, many ancient and holy buildings lay ruined and Chinese flags flew over Lhasa. The Chinese authorities announced to the world that Tibet had been 'liberated' and that the 'darkest feudal serfdom in the world' had been eliminated.

Following the Dalai Lama's flight into exile, the Chinese regression into Tibet continued unabated. During the period of the Cultural Revolution in China, these repressive measures were intensified by Mao to speed up the transition to a full communist society. In the first few years following the uprising, most of the monks and nuns were sent home and monasteries and nunneries closed. Monks and nuns were denounced as 'counter-revolutionaries' and targeted in 'struggle sessions'. The entire institutional framework of Buddhism in Tibet was forcibly dismantled. The inauguration of the Cultural Revolution in Tibet in 1966 marked the beginning of a complete assault on Tibetan society and culture. Under the banner of destroying the 'four olds' (old ideology, old culture, old customs, old habits), Tibetans were punished for deviating even slightly from the new proletarian culture exemplified by the Red Guards. In Tibet gangs of Red Guards moved across the country inflicting severe punishments including torture, gang rapes and wholesale executions. The Chinese systematically demolished much of Tibet's religious culture, plundering the monasteries of their valuables before razing them or turning them into stables or granaries. Any display of religion was prohibited, the practice of religion for both lay and clergy alike survived only in memory. The renewed practice of Buddhism did not begin until the end of the Cultural Revolution and the implementation of Deng Xiaoping's reform policies in Tibet after 1979. China's activities in Tibet were condemned by numerous international human rights organizations and Deng Xiaoping, who succeeded Mao after the latter's death in 1976, admitted that mistakes had been made in the suppression of Tibet by China. In the aftermath of the Cultural Revolution, Chinese policy in Tibet became more conciliatory. Tibet was proving to be expensive to hold securely, and Chinese indoctrination policies had not produced the desired results. Also, China, becoming concerned about world opinion, likely viewed the Dalai Lama and his Tibetan government in exile as an embarrassment. Travel restrictions were relaxed, prisoners were released and fact-finding missions sent by the Dalai Lama were allowed to tour Tibet.

When China admitted its mistakes in Tibet and allowed some freedom, one of the first spontaneous acts of the Tibetan people was to rebuild their monasteries all over Tibet, young men and women began renouncing their lay status and seeking ordination as monks and nuns. But the Chinese allowed only such religious practises as would impress the tourists who were allowed into Tibet. A new policy of moving in thousands of Han Chinese into Tibet was begun in 1984 and continues to this day. The Dalai Lama does not conceal his anxiety: 'Today Tibet is directly threatened in its national identity: dumping a mass of Chinese colonists on our territory involves a threat to the native population of assimilation and absorption…according to official Chinese statistics, the region of Koko Nor, in north eastern Tibet, where I was born, now contains nearly three million Chinese for 700,000 Tibetans…if the present policy goes on, soon Tibet will no longer be Tibet. We Tibetans have nothing against the Chinese. All we ask is what belongs to us by right.' A transnational political movement specifically focused on the political situation inside Tibet, with Tibetan independence as its goal, emerged since the outbreak of renewed protest inside Tibet in the autumn of 1987. Three demonstrations took place in the centre of Lhasa, the Tibetan capital, by the monks of the nearby Drepung and Sera monasteries. As protest has continued inside Tibet, virtually every religious act has assumed political significance. In October 1989, at a time when martial law was in force in Lhasa and overt political demonstrations were impossible, residents poured into Barkhor, to celebrate the award of the Nobel Peace Prize to the Dalai Lama, by burning juniper branches in incense burners. At first the authorities took no notice of the celebration, since it fell within the bounds of traditional religious practice and the crowd did not display the Tibetan flag or chant independence slogans. But as the Chinese government denounced the Nobel Peace Prize awarded to the Dalai Lama, the security forces were instructed to arrest the incense burners and public religious observances in monasteries were forbidden without permission. As the incidents of protests by monks and nuns increased in the period since 1990s, the exercise of political control over the monasteries has become stricter. Continuing political interference in the life of the monasteries and period expulsions have forced thousands of monks and nuns to flee to India during the 1990s.

At the time when he was attempting to practise the difficult balancing act of cohabitation with Communist China, between 1950 and 1959, despite his youth and political inexperience the Dalai Lama was cautiously exploring ways of possible change. Along with his countrymen he was caught unaware by the invader, time and history. The brutality of the succeeding upheaval will have cost his country and people very dear, moulding the shape of a different future.

8
The XIV Dalai Lama—In Exile and Beyond

AT AROUND 4 P.M. ON 31 MARCH 1959, the Dalai Lama dismounted from the dzomo [a female hybrid of a yak bull and a common cow], walked across a clearing in no man's land and was greeted by a Gurkha Commander bearing a traditional white scarf. He accepted the scarf and stepped across the Indian border and into exile. The uprising in 1959 against the Chinese presence in central Tibet involved many hundreds of monks, who took up arms to protect the Dalai Lama as he fled to India along with thousands of Tibetans. Nearly 50 years later, the Dalai Lama, still lives in exile, only a few days' travel from where he first arrived in India, along with those of the Tibetan community who made the long trek to freedom.

After the audacious escape of the Dalai Lama, assisted in its success by the willing sacrifice of many Tibetans, there were outbreaks of rioting throughout Lhasa which were brutally put down by the Chinese. Tens of thousands of Tibetans fled their country, leaving their homes, families, friends and majority of their possessions and followed their leader into an unknown future in exile. Many never survived the flight into exile; Chinese soldiers indiscriminately shot those caught in their attempts of fleeing; the perilous trek through the high mountain passes, walking through deep snow and blizzards, claimed more lives, especially those of children and old people. Many of those who did manage to make the crossover into India arrived depleted of physical strength and full of despair due to the loss of much more than their homeland.

Despite the fact that the Tibetans are a hardy race, they had up till now remained unexposed to other climates and lands, living in isolation on 'the roof of the world'. Upon their arrival in India, they were coerced to engage in a battle of a different kind, for which they were ill-equipped. They had to face a horde of unfamiliar diseases along with the rigours of a low-altitude climate. Many succumbed to the diseases common to tropical climates like, T.B. and digestive disorders of various kinds in addition to malnutrition and illness caused by the humid heat of the fast approaching Indian summer.

There was news of hundreds of Tibetans crossing over into India, Nepal and Bhutan, bringing with them little else except horrific tales of the battle in Lhasa. The Indian government, unprepared for such a massive influx of refugees, was swamped under the task of accommodating hundreds of these homeless, hapless peoples. Yet transit camps soon sprouted in Misamari and Baxa Duar to rehabilitate the refugees. Nehru meanwhile engaged himself in attempting to find a solution with the Chinese, refusing however to intervene, despite the criticisms of his fellow politicians. His predicament was delicate and difficult in the face of a mighty neighbour, whom he could ill afford to antagonize. However his humanitarian principles prevailed and he provided, as best as he could, the exiles with the bare essentials to rebuild their lives in alien lands and climes.

By June 1959 the refugees numbered more than 20,000 and swelled daily by new arrivals. The Dalai Lama held a meeting with Nehru in Delhi, in order to decide how best to proceed with the process of accommodating the increasing numbers of exiles, because the transit camps began overflowing with them, many of whom were ill and dying. The newly formed Tibetan government in exile, though officially unrecognized by the Indian government, had discussed with the Indian officials, a plan to employ the refugees in building roads in the north. These road camps were situated at a higher altitude, where the Tibetan people would be more comfortable, whereas the road building work would also allow them to earn a living or subsistence.

By now the number of refugees had risen to 30,000 and along with the rising numbers, arose another pressing concern; many of the refugees were monks and high lamas, the religious persecution in Tibet having affected them the most. They arrived with as many sacred texts as they could carry in an attempt to save them from annihilation. However, these monks too were indiscriminately set to work on road building. This propelled Nehru to ask various states of India to donate some land to the Tibetans to allow them to build their own communities. The first offer of 3,000 acres was made by the Karnataka state government, near Mysore in South India.

Many of the first 666 settlers at Bylakupee, in South India burst into tears on their arrival in December 1960. Supplied with tents and a few basic tools, they were then left to clear the jungle and to try to make farmland and build villages. The enormity of the task was finally matched by the indomitable Tibetan spirit and the encouragement of the Dalai Lama. However life was grim due to the unbearable heat, wild animals, particularly elephants, which rampaged periodically through the settlements.

At an interval of six months, 500 new settlers were sent down to Bylakupee. As the numbers of settlers grew, so did agriculture and small trades, improving their living conditions. By 1962 the first permanent living residences were completed; a decade or so later, there were 20 villages and six monasteries housing 10,000 people. This speaks volumes of the tenacity and ingenuity of the Tibetan people. Subsequently other settlements in eastern India in Kalimpong, Orrisa and Andhra Pradesh were established. On 30 April 1960, the Dalai Lama and his entourage arrived at Dharamshala, in the northern state of Himachal Pradesh, a place where the British took their summer vacations, being set on the side of the foothills of the Himalayas. Realizing that the Tibetan culture and the Tibetan race itself were in danger of extermination, Tibetan leaders began to plan for an indefinite future in exile. The new Tibetan refugee society began with a donation of land by the Indian government at a small township of McLeodganj in Dharamshala. This place has the Dhauladar range as a picturesque backdrop, with the snow clad peaks of this range being reminiscent of the home the refugees had left behind. Dharamshala soon became the administrative centre of the Tibetan community. The Tibetan government in exile now has a complex of buildings housing the offices of all its various departments, just around the corner from the library of the

Tibetan works and archives. As well as containing thousands of sacred texts and its own small publishing initiative, it houses a few priceless treasures that were rescued and smuggled over the mountains by the fleeing scholars.

The Dalai Lama successfully convinced the Indian government to fund a scholastic community of 1,500 monks, selected from the 6,000 who had escaped from Tibet. The refugee transit camp, Buxa Duar became Buxa Lama Ashrama. In 1963 the Dalai Lama brought together the heads of all the different Tibetan Buddhist traditions, as well as those of the Bon religion, in order to find common grounds for preserving their Tibetan culture. Soon thereafter The Dalai Lama re-established his own monastery, Namgyal, at Dharamshala. By 1968, the monasteries of Ganden, Drepung and Sera had been re-established in Karnataka. Gradually about 150 of the leading monastic traditions of Tibet have been rebuilt in India and the Himalayan countries.

Important centres of Tibetan culture soon established themselves at Dharamshala; the first was the Tibetan Dance and Drama Society. The Buddhist School of Dialectics helps keep the art of debating in the monastic communities vibrant. The Tibetan Medical Center which started out with three doctors, who managed to escape Tibet, had, by the early 1970s, graduated enough practitioners to staff the settlement communities. One of the more significant cultural institutions, begun in 1971, was the library of Tibetan Works and Archives, which has attracted Tibetan scholars worldwide. By 1984, the library had amassed 50,000 volumes of Tibet's literature, about 40 per cent of the total, the rest lost to the ravages of the Chinese troops.

Perhaps because of their shared suffering, the exiles realized that co-operative action was necessary for survival. As a result they shared resources and equipment, allowing the communities to maximize their ability to produce goods and render services. They also discovered the power of collective purchasing and marketing. In addition, the Tibetan penchant for trade proved to be an asset, and many Tibetans today make substantial profits from selling a wide range of goods. Though a few, with cynical attitudes, raise objections about the astounding success of the refugee communities which have been founded by penniless, displaced people in a foreign country, in general however, the refugees having displayed remarkable adaptability, have earned the admiration of the host countries.

Over the years McLeodganj has become 'Little Tibet', with more than 5,000 Tibetans living in the immediate area. Although Dharamshala has become the centre of the Tibetan community in exile, the majority of the Tibetan refugees live in other parts of India as well. Dharamshala perched on the steep sides of a mountain, has limited habitable space and few areas suitable for agriculture. In order to create self-sustaining Tibetan communities, the Indian government offered to lease uninhabited land in the southern state of Karnataka, which today houses the bulk of the refugee population.

Provision of education for the many refugee children was an essential that both Nehru and the Dalai Lama agreed and stressed upon. Nehru took personal interest in setting up and funding of separate schools for the Tibetan children. In addition to acting as agencies for the preservation of Tibetan culture, these schools would provide a platform for the Tibetan children to become part of the international mainstream. The first school was extablished with these intentions in Mussorie with 50 children. The Indian government created the Tibetan Schools Society as a separate branch of the Indian Ministry of Education. Tibetan children would receive Tibetan education in their own schools, and the curriculum also included subjects that would prepare them to participate in life of the modern society. Initially the Dalai Lama felt that education should be directed towards vocational training, but very soon many Tibetan children were qualifying for higher academic studies. To facilitate this process, the Institute of Higher Tibetan Studies was established in Sarnath, near Varanasi, in 1968. Most of the university trained Tibetan's have been absorbed into the Dalai Lama's administrative service. Opportunities to study abroad for several hundreds of Tibetans have assisted in broadening the outlook of the Tibetan exile community.

The Dalai Lama did much to restructure the government, with a return to Tibet clearly in mind. The notion of a political movement for Tibetan independence that incorporates both modern political ideas of freedom and human rights along with the central values of Buddhism is largely the creation of the present Dalai Lama. A guest of Nehru, and surrounded by the political environment of democratic India, with its own legacy of colonial rule and an independence movement, the Dalai Lama early on came to see the struggle for Tibetan independence in a similar light. In 1963, using socialist principles as guidelines, the Dalai Lama oversaw the drafting of a new constitution for the Tibetan government. It provided for a popularly elected legislature, which included men and women, from each province, and one cleric from each of the major sects, including Bon. One member, who distinguished himself in the Tibetan community, was appointed by the Dalai Lama. The Dalai Lama, who stood at the head of the government, appointed the cabinet under whom a number of departments worked. The constitution also renounced war, provided for universal suffrage, equality before law, freedom of religion, speech and assembly, the state ownership of land and a prohibition against the amassing of wealth. The Dalai Lama could also be impeached by a two-thirds vote of the legislature in the new constitution of Tibet. All Tibetans in the exile community vigorously opposed this clause, but the Dalai Lama insisted that no one should be above the law. The Dalai Lama has on a number of occasions suggested to remove himself from a direct political role in the Tibetan government, turning over the exercise of power to the democratically elected representatives.

Despite their apparent prosperity and seeming contentment, some of the young Tibetans have become disillusioned about ever returning to the land they have never known. The life of a refugee is understandably difficult for the generation that fled from their homeland, but there is now a whole new generation of young Tibetans who have never seen their country and who have different problems to overcome. Unemployment, lack of opportunity, and bleak future, relying mostly on selling Tibetan artifacts, is seeing the rise of a frustrated Tibetan youth. Recreational drug habits are creeping into the Tibetan culture. Just as in the 1960s angry youth of Europe and America were rebelling against restrictive culture, today's Tibetan youth feels limited and alienated due to their refugee status. The hope that they will one day return to a free Tibet is still alive in the dreams of the Tibetan exiles, but there are no longer rumours that prevailed several years ago, and it is not talked about as much as it used to be. The Land of the Snows remains at the centre of the Dalai Lama's worries. The Dalai Lama has painfully witnessed the upheavals which have affected The Roof of the World during recent decades, he is well aware that the past is past, and incidentally he makes it clear that in any case it would not be desirable to return to structures now decidedly superseded.

Despite being officially refugees, their government unrecognized, their country not acknowledged as being independent, the Tibetan's have still managed to survive extremely well in exile, some individuals having even become quite prosperous. They are also managing to preserve much of their cultural and spiritual heritage in exile. This survival is largely due to the skill of the Dalai Lama, his international status and high profile, guaranteeing international aid and ensuring the condemnation of the human rights abuses that continue in Tibet. The Dalai Lama continues to speak out about the plight of the Tibetan people and the Chinese occupation of Tibet at every opportunity. During the first years of his exile, other than his earlier visit to China, the Dalai Lama had not visited any country except India. But in 1967 he took his first trip abroad visiting Japan and Thailand. However the problem of the role in which he should be invited to these countries arose, in order not to compromise the country concerned in its diplomatic and trade relationships with China. The Chinese government subsequently attempted to prevent the Dalai Lama from engaging in any formal meetings with foreign government officials, saying that this would be construed as an intervention in its internal affairs. This edict is still in place today, which means that when the Dalai Lama visits another country, he is either a religious teacher or conference delegate or spokesperson on peace. Since the Tibetan government in exile is not recognized by the majority of the countries that he visits, he cannot discuss anything political with foreign government officials and often does not meet them publicly unless that country's leading religious leader is also present.

For six weeks in 1973, the Dalai Lama toured Europe, visiting 11 countries and encountering western culture for the first time. In Rome he met Pope Paul VI and was delighted to find that they agreed on the importance of his religious beliefs, whatever the creed. In Switzerland he met the early orphaned Tibetan exiles adopted by the Swiss families. Finally in 1979 he visited the U.S. to the greeting of 'Hello Dalai' on the front page headline of the New York Times. He returns to countries where he spoke a few years ago about the urgency to help the situation in Tibet, yet there has been little change. The same dedicated faces greet him and renew their pledges of support, but they are unable to coerce their governments into taking constructive action. Tibet support groups stage demonstrations, hold benefit concerts, and send out news letters but to little practical effect. President Bill Clinton had suggested that he would take a tougher stance with regard to the Chinese government and then renewed its 'most favoured nation' status without negotiating the issue of human rights.

It is thus obvious that the Chinese occupation of Tibet is a delicate political issue that has no simple solution. Despite this the Dalai Lama speaks on the Tibetan situation, he displays total commitment to his cause. He welcomes any dialogue with the Chinese though little is forthcoming. He is evidently saddened and tired by the situation, yet he speaks with passion and equanimity – even humor – and inspires people wherever he goes. During Buddhist teaching sessions, public talks and conferences, he spontaneously speaks about the situation; it is never far from his mind, 'For over 40 years Tibet has known a time of great suffering. I am therefore at present invested with an immense moral responsibility and not only towards the people of Tibet. I also have a duty, whenever I encounter someone who is interested in Tibet to explain the situation clearly and give an indication of what we are doing to resolve the problem. From the time of the occupation, 40 years ago the Chinese have used diverse methods at different times. Since the mid-fifties they have destroyed countless monasteries and temples; they have eliminated educated people, lay followers as well as monks, by imprisoning them, sending them to labour camps, or even executing them in public. Then there was the Cultural Revolution. Finally there was propaganda claiming that Tibetan culture is completely backward and obscure; it was said to be cruel and worthless and everything Tibetan was completely useless and uninteresting. But now things have changed. In the methods used now, since the mid-eighties, the official position is that Tibetan culture is an ancient culture, worthy of interest and must be preserved. The Chinese have put some signs in Tibet, up in the streets, and they have ordered

Chinese people living in Tibet to learn Tibetan. But underneath all of this the emphasis remains on Chinese studies, and in school examinations, for example, it is one's knowledge of China that matters. The traditional degree course is very serious and very long, requiring from 20 to 30 years to complete. There is no place in Tibet where these studies may be undertaken. As a result the level of traditional instruction in Tibet has dropped very low. For this reason, thousands of young people have no choice other than come to India to study at the monastic institutions set up in exile. So despite all the propaganda the reality has been a deliberate effort to eliminate our culture. And it is primarily due to the invasion of Chinese colonists that the cultural genocide is now occurring in Tibet.

'My opinion is that since everybody belongs to this world, we must try to adopt a good attitude worldwide, a good feeling for our fellow brothers and sisters. In my particular case, we Tibetans are carrying on a struggle for our rights. Some say that the Tibetan situation is only political, but I feel it is not. We Tibetans have a unique and distinct cultural heritage, just as the Chinese culture which spans so many centuries. Though we have deep respect and are not anti-Chinese, we six million Tibetans have an equal right to maintain our own distinctive culture as long as we do not harm others. Materially we are backward, but in spiritual matters—in terms of development of the mind—we are quite rich. We Tibetans are Buddhists and the Buddhism we practise is rather complete form of Buddhism. Also we have kept it active and very much alive in our daily practises.

In the past century we remained a peaceful nation with our unique culture. Now, unfortunately, during the last few decades, this nation and its culture are being deliberately destroyed. We like our own culture, our own land; we have the right to preserve it. Also the six million Tibetan people are human beings, no matter we are a materially backward country or not. We are six million human souls with the right to live as human beings. This is the problem.

I am serving our cause with the motivation of service to humankind, not for reasons of power, not out of hatred. Not just as a Tibetan but as a human being, I think it is worthwhile to preserve that culture, that nation, to contribute to the world society. This is why I am persistent in our movement, and though some people see it as a purely political matter, I know it is not. We hope that the overall attitude of the People's Republic of China is changing, but we are cautious due to our past experiences. I do not say this out of a wish to criticize, rather it is a fact.' – 'Compassion in Global Politics' (Los Angeles World Affairs Council).

Perhaps the central platform in the Dalai Lama's efforts towards reconciliation with China is his Five-Point Peace Plan, which he first outlined in an address to the United States Congress in 1987. It comprises the following: 1) the transformation of Tibet into a zone of peace 2) abandonment of China's population transfer policy 3) respect for human rights and democratic freedom in Tibet 4) removal of China's nuclear weapon programme and nuclear waste facilities from Tibet and 5) negotiations on Tibet's status and relations between the peoples of China and Tibet. The following year, in a speech to the European Parliament in Strasbourg, the Dalai Lama offered Beijing the option of retaining control over foreign affairs and defence in Tibet in exchange for Tibetan autonomy in matters of civil administration, religion, education, trade, culture, tourism and science. While the Chinese response to these overtures was to denounce them, which in turn triggered the 1987 and 1989 demonstrations in Lhasa, the world's response was more positive; in 1989 the Dalai Lama was awarded the Nobel Peace prize. Not all the Tibetan exile community has agreed with the Dalai Lama regarding his conciliatory approach to China. In turn the Dalai Lama explained his reasons for relinquishing the demand for independence thus: 'at the end of 1978 the Chinese government made it known that it wanted to establish contact with me. I immediately responded and sent a special envoy, one of my brothers, who speaks Chinese well. He met Deng Xiaoping. They conferred for an hour and Deng Xiaoping told him that he could talk about everything except total independence, but that was a considerable condition.

Since then, in the 14 years which have followed, my entire approach has been based on that condition. That is why I do not ask for complete independence. This does not mean that we do not have the right to demand independence. Everyone now knows that Tibet is an occupied country. I generally refer to my way of proceeding as the Middle Way. I stated very clearly in my proposition at Strasbourg that the final decision belongs to the Tibetan people themselves. Some Tibetans were very critical of this proposition, some going so far as to say to me, "You the Fourteenth Dalai Lama, have sold the birthright of the Tibetan people!" but I think that we must face the situation squarely: Tibet is a landlocked country; to gain access to the sea we are obliged to rely on a neighbouring country. In the present context, it seems fairer and more realistic to try and come up with an arrangement or a solution with the Chinese.' However frustration is mounting among the Tibetans of the younger generation, both within Tibet and outside of it, regarding the Dalai Lama's moderate approach in the pursuance of the issue of Tibet's liberation. Some of the more radical Tibetans in exile are in favour of reviving the armed guerrilla movement within Tibet. The Dalai Lama completely denounces such extreme measures by saying, 'I absolutely refuse the use of violence. For several years now I have been asked on several occasions what I would do if the despair of certain Tibetans drove them to violence, and I have always replied that if that were to happen I would give up and step back. I have reasons for thinking in this way; it is not merely a blind belief. First of all, I believe the basic nature of human beings is gentle and compassionate. It is therefore in our own interest to encourage that nature, to make it live within us, to leave room for it to develop. If on the contrary we use violence, it is as if we voluntarily obstruct the positive side of human nature and prevent its evolution.

The First World War ended with the defeat of Germany, and this defeat left a deep trauma in the German people. That is how the seeds of the Second World War were sown. Once violence gains the upper hand in a situation, emotions can no longer be controlled. This is dangerous and leads to tragedy.

Many Chinese people now express sympathy for our cause and as a result are openly demonstrating their support for Tibet's struggle for independence. It is precisely for this reason that many nations are now offering more vigorous support than before. I often tell my people that having practiced non-violence in choosing a democratic system for Tibet's future does not constitute an end in itself, but must serve as an example for the entire world. To seek peace with non-violence is to ally intelligence and skilful means.'

Perhaps it is because the Dalai Lama is first of all, the Buddhist monk Tenzin Gyatso, that his actions in the secular sphere are informed by his spiritual understanding, 'I feel personally that the Tibetan issue in which I am involved is actually a struggle for the survival of spirituality, of human values....the preservation of the Tibetan culture and Buddhism itself, is not only for the benefit of 6 million Tibetans;..... humanity itself is benefited by this tradition and culture.'

Before making any other assessment, it is vital to define the misunderstanding that underlies the disagreement between Tibet and China. By their history, culture and tradition, the two countries are inevitably neighbours; nature has made it so. Politically, however, they have always represented two distinct entities, even if in centuries of fluctuating interplay, links of a specific nature have grown between them. The kernel of the tragedy is unquestionably to be found in the Chinese wish to impose the image of a factitious similarity, while the Tibetan determination to display its radical otherness has not weakened, and on the contrary has been reinforced, with the passing years. Certainly there is a real danger for the Roof of the World to being submerged by the influx of wave after wave of Chinese colonists in search of living space, but forced assimilation has never been a viable, long-term solution in human history, short of accepting the physical disappearance of a community too numerically weak to stand in the way of the invader.

The one question that has most frequently been posed to the Dalai Lama in every conference or council, in every country he has visited is regarding the continuance of the institution of the Dalai Lamas after him. The Dalai Lama has answered this question many times, in the same way to different people; 'The question has been raised several times, especially since 1979. That is because at that time there were some who seemed to think that it was a topical matter, at the moment when the Chinese were doing their utmost to put it about that there was no Tibetan problem, and that the only point at issue was the Dalai Lama. They assured anyone who would listen that the Tibetans were very happy in Tibet since their liberation by the Chinese, and that the sole obstacle to their continued happiness was the Dalai Lama, whose only purpose was to restore his own authority and to regain his former privileges....the question has nothing to do with the institution as such, and if pushed, I would even go so far as to say that it is not particularly my business; personally it does not affect me. The situation is changing, and if circumstances make the historic institution irrelevant, if there is no longer any need for it, and its role in history is over and done with, then never mind, there is no harm in putting an end to it...Tibet is perfectly conceivable without a Dalai Lama: it lasted for a very long time before the institution existed as such, and in theory it is completely possible...for the moment, of course, the Dalai Lama is a symbol, a symbol of Tibet. That is why he is so important for the Tibetan nature and culture.'

In an interview to Gill Farrer Halls in 1998 the Dalai Lama says this:

GFH: In a recent statement you said if the Tibetan issue remains unresolved and the Tibetans still want a Dalai Lama you would reincarnate outside Tibet. What are the implications of this?

DL: 'For many years I have said this….in any case, if during my lifetime, the return to Tibet does not materialize, the Tibetan people want me to continue and I pass away outside Tibet as a refugee, then logically if it is wanted, the reincarnation will appear outside because the purpose of the reincarnation is to continue the tasks started by the previous life which have not yet been accomplished. So in my life as XIV Dalai Lama, I started some work, like the freedom struggle, which is not yet fulfilled, so the task of the next reincarnation is to continue that work.

So if the next reincarnation comes inside Tibet and in case the Chinese manipulate that situation, then this becomes the destroyer of the work started by the XIV Dalai Lama. Then politically, some Chinese officials have expressed that the whole Tibet issue relies very much on one person. This person is now getting older and older and once this person has passed away, we will choose another young Dalai Lama. Then there will be no future for the Tibetan struggle. This happened as early as the 1980s, so this is a foolish calculation by the Chinese officials.'

It is not at all easy to raise these delicate questions with the Tibetans. From the humblest to the least directly concerned, inside and outside the country, and from the nearest and the farthest, from the focal point where the Sovereign of the Land of Snows now lives, there is no disputing the unanimous view that the Dalai Lama is Tibet. No matter how hard he may try to remove himself from the issue, and to convince his fellow countrymen that it is an open question, this is one issue on which they appear to be unwilling to follow him. An Indian journalist, a grandson of Mahatma Gandhi, once said of the XIV Dalai Lama, and said rightly, that he was 'the gift of providence to Tibet, and the gift of Tibet to the world'. By forcefully adhering to the struggle to preserve the values of the religious culture which he personifies, the present Dalai Lama has successfully led the struggle to preserve Tibetan Buddhist culture. That this success has grown into a worldwide dissemination of Tibetan Buddhist spirituality and concurrent concern for the fate of Tibet itself is largely due to the personality and prestige of the Dalai Lama and, by extension, the institution he personifies. As the institution of the Dalai Lama is representative of one of the great traditional wisdoms bequeathed to human society we can all hope it continues to serve the growing constituency it represents.

9

Of Buddha—A Life Less Ordinary

OSHO ON BUDDHA: 'he is not the founder of Buddhism—Buddhism is a by product—but he is the beginner of a totally different kind of religion in the world. He's the founder of a religionless religion. He has propounded not religion but religionlessness. And this is a great radical change in the history of human consciousness.

Before Buddha there were religions but never a pure religionlessness. Man was not yet mature. With Buddha humanity enters into a mature age. All human beings have not yet entered into that, that's true, but Buddha has heralded the path, Buddha has opened the gateless gate. It takes time for human beings to understand such a deep message. Buddha's message is the deepest ever. Nobody has done the work Buddha has done, the way he has done. Nobody else represents pure fragrance' (Diamond Sutra).

The Buddha Sakyamuni was a historical sage who worked out his own peace by his own efforts and methods of spiritual 'sadhana' (meditation). The Buddha's Nirvana was that very state of peace described by his predecessors. Buddha after his enlightenment wanted to share his bliss of peace with all beings, who were subject to suffering and sorrows. So his universal prayer was: 'Sabbe satta sukhita hotu', may all beings be happy. His command to his monk disciples was to move around the world, 'for good of many, for happiness of many', 'bahujana hitaya bahujana sukahaya'. The Buddhist ideal, since the time of the Buddha, is being materialized with this dictum 'good and happiness' for all.

The doctrine of the Buddha, the aim of happiness and peace for an individual and for all, is being revalued, reconsidered and realized in a new perspective since the later part of the last century of the Christian era. Gautama, having become Buddha, taught for a period of 45 years and when he was 80 years old, passed into Nirvana. Then as time went on the historicity of his personality became fainter in the minds of the people and idealization began, till at last Gautama was regarded as a superhuman. This idealization consisted of two points: firstly the early Buddhists, abiding by the law of cause and effect, traced the cause of Gautama's attainment of Buddha-hood from the past, beyond his life in this world. The superiority of Gautama Buddha, they speculated must be the result not only of his excellent practises in this world but also of the merits he accumulated in previous existences.

In the words of Bhikshu (monk) Sangharakshita, 'The human and historical biography of Gautama Buddha is the story of the mystic marriage of the human and the divine, the individual and the universal, the terrestrial and the cosmic, the immanent urge and the transcendental ideal'.

By Buddha, at first, was meant a great teacher. Then he was treated as a superman and raised to the level of a superhuman, transcendental being. The next step of development was to regard Buddha as a 'Principle', the ultimate reality. Then it was believed that the Buddha, the ultimate reality, is not something external that has to be achieved or attained but a potential ability, called Buddha-nature, that has to be awakened. And this Buddha-nature is inherent not only in human beings but also in every specific being and in every concrete matter.

In the sixth century BC, religion was forgotten in India. The lofty teachings of the Vedas were thrown in the background. There was much priest-craft everywhere. The insincere priests traded on religion. They duped the people in a variety of ways and amassed wealth. They propounded meaningless rituals which included brutal sacrifice of animals in the name of religion, and the innocent and unsuspecting populace followed them faithfully. The caste system was used to categorize, discriminate and manipulate people according to their professions. In the backdrop of such cruelty, ethical degeneration and unrighteousness, the Buddha took birth.

Little is known of the life of the Buddha; the legend is the foundation of Buddhist understanding and practice. Queen Maya, long childless, dreamt during the midsummer festival that a superb white elephant, bearing in his silver trunk a white lotus flower, came to her, struck her side gently with a flower, and disappeared. The king Suddhodana, Gautama's father was overjoyed at the dream, and the queen conceived. When her time came, on her way to her family home, she stopped at the Lumbini pleasure grove, full of flowers and alive with sweet birds. She reached up and grasped a Sal tree, and the baby was delivered through her right side. The baby's body showed the 32 Good Omens, including the spot of fine hair between the eyebrows, fine black body hair growing upwards on the glowing, golden skin, small prints of wheels on the soles of the feet and long earlobes. It was prophesied by the Brahmin Atisa: 'The child, on attaining manhood, would become either a universal monarch (Chakravartin), or, abandoning the house and home, would assume the robe of a monk and become a Buddha, a perfectly enlightened soul, for the salvation of the mankind'. The king asked, 'What shall my son see to make him retire from the world?' The astrologer replied, 'Four signs'.

'What four?' asked the king.

'A decrepit old man, a diseased old man, a dead man and a monk – four will make the prince retire from the world,' replied the astrologer.

As the child grew, the father attempted to shield him. The young Siddharatha was the perfect prince; he was good at military exercises and sports and at his father's knee showed acumen at the law and helped judge disputes. Once, however, at the annual rite, when the king ceremonially ploughed the fields, the child was left under a tree, and there he experienced his first meditative trance.

King Suddhodana feared that he might lose his son, so he attempted to attach the latter to earthly objects by seeping him in sense pleasures, surrounding him with beautiful maidens, gardens, fountains, palaces, music and dances. At 19 he was given or chose a wife, princess Yashodhara. A garden of delight was under construction, where no touch of morality could be seen, but on the carefully swept and decorated road, one untoward sight, by the intent of the gods, escaped the vigil of the king's officers: 'a man wasted by age, with decayed teeth and grey hair, bent and broken down in body,' say the Jataka tales. The prince's charioteer, Channa, explained to the prince, that to everyone who was born, old age must come. Soon the prince rode out into the town and saw, a diseased man and a corpse, greatly increasing his agitation. 'Once again, when the future Buddha, as he was going to his pleasure ground, saw one who had abandoned the world, of composed mien, and simply clad, he asked his charioteer, "Friend, what kind of man is that?" "The mendicant, a sannyasi". And thus the four omens were fulfilled, and the future Buddha cherished the thought of renouncing the world'. This resolution of his son, was vehemently opposed by his father and the courtiers.

About this time, Yashodhara bore a son. Gautama or Siddharta (the name given to him by his parents) then aged 29 and pondering his future course said, 'An impediment, a fetter (Rahula) has come into being'. So the son was named Rahula.

The prince entered the palace to the usual singing and dancing by women as beautiful as celestial nymphs, but he was pensive, ignored the entertainers and fell asleep. 'And the future Buddha awoke and perceived these women lying asleep, with their musical instruments scattered around them on the floor, some with their bodies wet and trickling phlegm and spittle, some grinding their teeth and muttering in their sleep, and some with their dresses fallen apart to disclose their loathsome nakedness'. Surfeited with sensual pleasures, he saw that magnificent palace as a charnel house full of corpses, and the three modes of existence—the world of passion, the world of form and the world without form—seemed like houses afire.

Thus the very means that his father took to entangle him more deeply in pleasures, ironically strengthened his resolve to leave the house in search of emancipation.

He resolved to accomplish the Great Renunciation, that very day. He called Channa, to saddle the horse, Kanthaka. Then he went to meet his son. But asleep with his mother, the infant's face was hidden by Yashodhara's hand. Gautama, fearing that if he saw his son, his resolve might weaken, left the palace without waking up his wife and seeing his son.

He left the city with Channa; the gods assisted him by muffling the hoofs of the horse, so that no one would hear him ride away. After they were at a safe distance from the city, the prince stopped, gave his ornaments to Channa, bade him return to his father alone with the weeping horse, Kanthaka. Thereon he proceeded on foot to Rajagriha, cut off his long hair, which were a sign of a Kshatriya (warrior) ruler, changed his rich robes for those of a hunter, and begged for food.

During his quest to find out about the miseries of life, he was fortunate to have met with and studied under two famous teachers of the day—Arada Kalama, who taught him the various stages of meditation and Udraka Ramaputra, who explained to him the dualistic interpretation of the Veda. However, his spirit yet remained unquenched. Nowhere could he find the object of his search—an escape from the miseries and vanities of life into a condition from which no return to life and its troubles was possible. 'I search', he said, 'for that which is imperishable and permanent'. He seemed to be inextricably entangled in an existence in which everything was subject to the ceaseless rotation of decay, death and birth.

So he moved on from Rajagriha to a pleasant grove at Uruvela, where he met five ascetics. With them he philosophized and practised traditional brahaminical austerities. For the next six years he sought liberation through yoga, until the severe physical austerities left him extremely weak in body and he fainted and fell to the ground. When he came to his senses, he decided, 'These austerities are not the way to enlightenment'. Just at that time, some dancing girls were passing by and joyfully singing a song which caught the attention of Gautama. Although, for the girls the song held no deep meaning, but Gautama extracted from it a profound spiritual message.

'Fair goes the dancing when the sitar is tuned,
tune us the sitar neither high nor low
and we will dance in the hearts of men.
The string overstretched breaks, the music dies,
the string over-slack is dumb and the music dies,
tune us the sitar neither high nor low'.

Buddha realized then that he should not go to extremes in torturing the body by starvation and that he should adopt the golden mean or the happy medium or the middle path by avoiding extremes. So when Sujata, a respectful young maiden, brought him a bowl of milk-rice, he accepted it. He was unmindful of the scorn of his five ascetic friends, who left him and proceeded to Benares. But he conceived the wisdom of the Middle Way between self-deceiving indulgence and self-mortifying austerity. And then Gautama proceeded on the path of enlightenment with a new insight.

He spread a mat of the 'Kusa' grass (the sacred grass of the Vedic rites) under a pipal tree (ficus religiosa) and he vowed:

'May, as long as I sit here, my body wither away,
may the skin, the bones and the flesh decay,
but until I have attained enlightenment
which is hard to be secured even during many eons-
I shall not move from this place.'

He applied the full powers of a mature man with trained intellect, a body disciplined in yoga and austerity and rich human experience. He knew social power, indulgence to surfeit in human pleasures, love of wife and child, and the vanity and evanescence of them all. His mind started with the beginning of his quest, his realization of man's sorrow, and worked back to an ultimate cause, which he found to be ignorance, man's misconceiving of his own image. Once he pierces through the basic human ignorance in bondage to desire, he can conceive of liberation, happiness beyond physical sensation, a state beyond the unending cycle of rebirth into mortal frustration.

He sat in a posture of meditation and rays of light poured forth from him, illuminating all worlds in all directions. Perceiving this overwhelming radiance, the demon Mara became alarmed, since he knew that this presaged the enlightenment of a Buddha. Gautama recovered consciousness only to fall prey to an agony of mental conflict, which legends depict fantastically, as an almost Miltonic picture of a battle between Mara and Gautama.

Mara in Buddhist mythology plays a role similar to the Satan in Christianity: he tempts people to perform evil actions, which lead to their downfall. Unlike the Satan, however, Mara primarily seduces people into ignorance, and not sin. Sin, in Buddhism, is a second-order problem, an outgrowth of ignorance. We only commit evil deeds because we fail to recognize that they inevitably rebound on us and cause suffering. More importantly, we think that selfish actions will result in personal happiness, but the only true happiness comes from the attainment of enlightenment. Mara's primary purpose is to blind people to these truths. The enlightenment of Buddha is the greatest tragedy of Mara, since Buddhas not only escape Mara's clutches, but through their compassionate activity they teach others the path to enlightenment, thus robbing Mara of countless victims.

Overwhelmed by terror and hatred of the incipient Buddha, Mara rushed to the circle of enlightenment to stop Gautama's ascension to Buddha-hood. With his screaming hordes of demons, Mara hurled missiles, rocks and other things at Gautama, who sat calmly absorbed in meditation. Through his yogic powers, everything Mara threw at him was transformed into flowers.

Enraged at his failure to even distract Gautama, Mara ordered his daughters to seduce him, but in vain. His powers transformed them into hideous hags, withered and ugly. Mara, undeterred, rallied his vast demon army for assaulting Gautama, who still sat unmoved and undistracted in his place of meditation. Remaining motionless, Gautama showed Mara a vision of the inevitable outcome of the attack: his forces routed and in disarray Mara himself humbled before Gautama. Mara was then shown a vision of his own old age and death, which so terrified him that he fled, together with all his host.

After defeating Mara, Gautama returned to single-pointed meditation. He, 'initiated energy, undeterred, attended to self-possession, not distracted, calmed his body, not excited, and concentrated his thoughts, focused on one point'. Distancing himself from all mundane attachments, he attained the first and second concentrations. He then surpassed them, entering into the third and fourth concentrations, each of which surpasses those below it. These, however, are merely mundane meditative attainments, and they only lead to rebirth in a blissful state, and not to enlightenment. Those who are reborn in this state must someday exhaust the karma that caused their happy rebirth and again return to the lower realms of cyclic existence, and so Buddhists traditionally have viewed them as a trap, since they only lead to a transitory state of happiness.

Gautama continued his meditation. During the first watch of the night, he realized that all things within cyclic existence are bound together by intersecting casual connections. He perceived how all beings are born, age and pass away under the influence of their past karma, and he fully comprehended the operations of the karma. At that time, he developed three of the distinctive powers of a Buddha: the power to create miraculous manifestations, the power of clairaudience, and the ability to know the thoughts of others.

During the second watch of the night, he acquired the three 'knowledges': he was able to know of all his previous births, he understood how beings transmigrate in accordance with their karma, and he comprehended the 'four noble truths', which were to become the corner stone of Buddhist practice.

In the third watch, he understood the causes of suffering and realized how suffering can be eliminated. According to the 'vinaya' (the texts which outline the rules for Buddhist monks and nuns), during the night of his enlightenment, his future attendant Ananda and his son Rahula were born.

At dawn he perfected his awareness and became a Buddha, a being who has eliminated even the subtlest traces of ignorance, who has become omniscient and, spontaneously, perfectly compassionate. At this point, however, the legendry histories speak of this eminence as one which no other man could attain, but it was a purely and confessedly human process by which he won his way to light. Buddha described the experiences of his 'samadhi': 'I thus behold my mind released from the defilement of earthly existence, released from the defilement of sensual pleasures, released from the defilement of heresy, released from the defilement of ignorance'. In the emancipated state arose the knowledge: 'I am emancipated, rebirth is extinct, the religious walk is accomplished, what had to be done is done, and there is no need for the present existence. I have overcome all foes; I am all-wise; I am free from stains in every way; I have left everything and have obtained emancipation by the destruction of desire. Myself having gained knowledge, whom should I call my master? I have no teacher; no one is equal to me. I am the holy one in this world; I am the highest teacher. I alone am the absolute omniscient one (Sambuddho). I have gained coolness by the extinction of all passion and have obtained Nirvana. To find the kingdom of law (Dharmo) I go to the city of Varanasi. I will beat the drum of immortality in the darkness of this world.'

How long he remained in the trance of enlightenment, of non-duality is lost in poetry, but afterwards he sat in joy, contemplating the fulfilment of his yearnings and his disciplines. Then he had to face the decision that was so fateful for mankind. Should he like many other Indian mystics retire from the world with his revelation, his mastery of Oneness, or should he go back among divided, stumbling men and try to teach them the way? Mara, his remnant of mortality, urged him to accept victory and Nirvana.

'I secured the cognition of the Truth, profound,

Free from defilement, illuminating, eternal, and like nectar.

But, if I should demonstrate it to others, they will not understand.

Therefore I shall abide in solitude in the forest'.

Even while thinking thus, he was reminded of his previous resolutions to work for the benefit of others, and he was moved by compassion for their sufferings, then Brahma, one of the great gods of the Indian pantheon, appeared before him and begged the Buddha to teach others so that they may free themselves from suffering. Buddha knew that most people would be utterly incapable of understanding the profundity of his teachings, but that there would be some exceptional individuals who would hear him and develop true realization. For their benefit, Buddha decided to devote himself to teaching.

Still absorbed in profound meditation on the final nature of reality, he considered where to begin his teaching career. He first thought of instructing his former teachers, Arada Kakama and Udraka Ramaputra, but his supra-normal perception revealed that they had already died. He then decided to teach his five former companions, who were practicing austerities in the deer park at Sarnath (near modern day Varanasi). But on seeing him, his former companions, viewing him as a weakling, who had been unable to endure the rigours of meditation, decided to avoid him. However, struck by his transformed persona, that radiated serenity and wisdom, they were tugged by compulsion to request him to reveal to them the Truth he had realized. Agreeing, he first immersed himself in meditation and then delivered his first sermon to his five companions, in the deer park at Sarnath. This is referred to as 'The Sutra Turning the Wheel of Dharma' because in this talk he set in motion a new cycle of teaching that would lead countless sentient beings to enlightenment.

After hearing this teaching, Kaundinya, one of the five ascetics, grasped the meaning of Buddha's words, overcame attachment, desire and ignorance and became the first 'Arhant' (one who will attain final Nirvana at the end of the present life as a result of eliminating mental afflictions and attachment to the world). The five ascetics asked to be accepted by Buddha as his disciples and thus began the 'sangha', the order of Buddhist monks and nuns.

Buddha then received a message from his father asking him to visit the latter, wanting to see him before he died. Accepting this invitation, he set out for Kapilvastu. On reaching he was thronged by his family in order to see him, but they were not pleased to see him in an ascetic's attire. Since they had made no arrangements for the daily food of his followers, he went to the city, begging from door to door. Pained by this his father tempted to stop him, to which Gautama replied, 'O king I am a mendicant. I am a monk. It is my duty to get alms from door to door. This is the duty of the order. Why do you stop this? The food that is obtained from alms is very pure.'

During his visit to Kapilvastu, all, save his wife, came to Gautama to pay him their respects. She believed, 'He himself will come to me if I am of any value in his eyes'. Since the day her husband had left, Yashodhara gave up all luxuries, ate simple food only once a day and slept on a mat. Hearing of this, Gautama was greatly moved and he went to see her. When Buddha prepared to leave the palace, Yashodhara told her son Rahula, 'O Rahula! That monk is your father. Go to him and ask for your birthright. Tell him boldly. "I am your son. Give me my heritage"'. Rahula did as instructed by his mother. Buddha did not reply but walked off into the forest with a persistent Rahula in tow. Upon reaching the forest, Buddha told one of his disciples, 'I give this boy the precious spiritual wealth I acquired under the sacred Bo-tree. I make him the heir to that wealth.' Thus Rahula was initiated into the order of monks. Of the vast number of discourses delivered by the Buddha, the majority of them were rendered at the two major cities of Rajagriha and Shravasti. From the time Buddha and his followers first went to live in Shravasti, it virtually became their headquarters. Of the discourses of the Buddha, which go to make the 'Sutta-Pitaka', 871 are said to have been delivered at Shravasti. Of 498 canonical Jataka stories, the telling of which is attributed to the Buddha, 416 are said to have been told at Shravasti. Twenty-five rainy seasons were spent there by the Buddha; the remaining 20 were spent in various other towns and cities.

After spending the rainy season at Sarnath with his disciples, Buddha began to travel, teaching anyone who asked. From Sarnath (in Varanasi), he travelled to another one of the six great cities of the time, Rajagriha—the capital of the great Magadhan empire. At Rajagriha he amassed more followers, including Sariputra and Moggallana, who later, along with Ananda, became the most prominent members of the order.

His stepmother, Prajapati, was so taken in by her stepson's teachings that she decided to renounce the world and follow him, but at that time there was no order of nuns. She travelled to meet the Buddha, and arrived exhausted and covered with dust. Then reverently she requested the Buddha to initiate an order of nuns for women aspiring enlightenment. But Buddha refused her request, advising her to pursue a virtuous life as a laywoman. Prajapati persisted but was repeatedly refused. Undeterred, she asked Ananda to intercede but to no avail. Buddha's refusal was not based on the denigration of the morals of women, their intelligence or their spiritual capabilities but rather on an understanding of interpersonal and intra-sexual relations. The monks who followed Buddha at that time had no monastic institutions and were a group of wandering celibate male ascetics who had renounced the world and its attachments. Buddha recognized that one of the strongest attachments is the desire for sexual gratification, and that placing men and women in close proximity, would inevitably lead to temptation. Finally, however, Buddha relented, agreeing that if he were to ordain nuns, if not all, at least some were bound to attain nirvana.

Buddha continued to travel and teach anyone who cared to listen and comprehend. He retired from the world at 29; spent six years in study and meditation prior to his appearance as a teacher, and for 45 years after that he lived a life of constant travelling, teaching and thinking. For 45 years he walked through the Ganges valley and indiscriminately preached to all—lay and religious, kings and subjects, rich and poor. The rainy season was spent in viharas—monasteries built for the order by wealthy lay adherents. In his wanderings during the nine months of good weather, the Buddha was accustomed to regularly walking 15-20mi. a day. He organized rules for the monks so that they would help each other put aside their false notions of individual soul entities, the major impediment to enlightenment. And when he died at 80, about 480 BC, he reminded them in his last words that all composite things (including men) are evanescent and that they should be lamps unto themselves and look out for their own spiritual welfare. When Ananda, his personal attendant, requested that he leave some final instructions for the community of monks, the Buddha replied thus:

'What does the community of monks expect of me Ananda? I have taught the doctrine without omission, without excluding anything. As to this, Ananda, the Tathagata [Buddha] is not a "close fisted teacher" with reference to the doctrine [i.e. he holds nothing back]. If anyone should think that he should watch over the community of monks or that the community of monks should refer to him, then, let him promulgate something about the community of monks. The Tathagata does not think that he should watch over the community of monks or they should refer to him…Ananda, I am now aged, old, an elder, my time has gone. I have arrived at the period of my life, which is 80 years. Just as an old cart is made to go by with bands, so I think the Tathagata's body is made to go by tying it together by bands. Ananda, on an occasion when the Tathagata by withdrawing his attention from all signs, by the cessation of some emotions, enters into sign-less concentration of thought and stays in it, on that occasion the Tathagata's body is made comfortable.

Therefore, Ananda....you should live with yourselves as islands, with yourselves as refugees, with no one else as refuge; with the doctrine as an island, with the doctrine as a refuge, with no one else as refuge.'

Shortly before his death, Buddha gathered his disciples, provided them with a set of guidelines concerning the authority of scriptures and then announced that the time of his nirvana was at hand. He instructed his students to cremate his body and build a reliquary monument for the remains. Though his grieving disciples attempted to persuade him to slightly delay his Nirvana, he assured them that he had taught them everything, without holding anything back. They had all they needed to attain liberation; they only needed to rely on their own efforts because in the final analysis each person decides his or her own fate, and liberation is gained through personal effort, not through intervention of another being. To Ananda he said:

'It might be that you would think, Ananda, that the teaching has lost its teacher, our teacher does not exist. You should not perceive things in this way. The doctrine and discipline that I have taught and described will be the teacher after me.'

He then delivered his final words to his disciples:

'Monks, all compounded things are subject to decay and disintegration. Work out your own salvations with diligence.'

These were the last words that the Buddha uttered, after which he entered into progressively higher meditative stages, until he completely transcended all worldly things and attained Nirvana.

During his many years of travelling and teaching, Buddha had enough time to thoroughly think out the views of life.

And by his constant intercourse with all the most cultured and earnest thinkers of the day extending through the large territory, stretching from Patna (in Bihar) in the south-east to Savatthi, in the north-west, about 300mi. long and 100mi. in breadth, he had frequent opportunities of comparing his views with those of such men.

Moreover, by mixing daily with men from all walks of life—kings, merchants, peasants, Brahmins—he was, with absolute clarity, able to comprehend the needs and aspirations, the hopes and fears of our common humanity.

It is an interesting evidence of the wonderful tolerance which prevailed at that time, through the valley of the Ganges, that a teacher, whose whole system was so diametrically opposed to the dominant creed and logically so certain to undermine the influence of the Brahmins, the parsons of the day, should, nevertheless, have been allowed to carry on his propaganda so ceaselessly and so peacefully through a considerable period of time. Wherever he went, it was the Brahmins themselves who took the most earnest interest in his speculations, even though he rejected many beliefs and rituals enshrined in the Vedas which the Brahmins propagated. Many of his chief disciples and some of the distinguished members of his order were Brahmins. In utter disregard of the caste system, he admitted men from all castes into his community. Even though there were individuals who foresaw that this breaking down of caste barriers would, in the long run, lower the social position and pecuniary advantages of the Brahmins, yet on the whole he was regarded by the Hindus as a Hindu. He suffered no persecution either during his lifetime or till many centuries later, for his divergent views. It is a striking result of the permanent effect which this spirit of toleration had, that the great Buddhist Emperor Ashoka, in his famous edicts, inculcated reverence to the Brahmins and to the teachers of the rival sects, as much as to the leaders of his own persuasion. Throughout the long history of Buddhism, which is the history of more than half the people of the world for 2,500 years, the Buddhists have uniformly been tolerant; and have appealed not to the sword, but to intellectual and moral suasion.

Despite his differences with the religion of the Vedas, Buddha was born and brought up as a Hindu and died as one too. His teachings, far-reaching and original as they were, and subversive of the religion of the day, were Indian throughout. Without the intellectual work of his predecessors his own work, however original, would have been impossible. He undoubtedly was the greatest of them all and the world has acknowledged him as the most intellectual of all religious teachers. But Buddhism is essentially an Indian system. The Buddha himself was, throughout his career, a characteristic Indian, the greatest and wisest of the Hindus. However, there are some who vociferously disagree about Buddha having inherited the Hindu religious system. And their argument in this matter has a strong basis: it is an anachronism, they believe, to ascribe a Hindu religious tradition to that early period; the characteristic set of beliefs and practices which came to be known as 'Hindu' was yet to be developed. Moreover considering Buddha's unacceptability of the authority of the Vedas, disbelief in God and the theories of creation, it cannot be believed that he was heir to the Hindu tradition. It has been suggested that if Gautama was indebted to any earlier figure in the cultural history of India, the most likely is Kapila, to whom is attributed the atheistic Samakhya doctrine.

Following Buddha's death, his disciples collected all his instructions. The teachings of the Hinayana were collected by 500 of his disciples and arranged into three groups or 'baskets'. These were the abhidharma (philosophy), the vinaya (monastic conduct) and the sutras (discourses of the Buddha). The teachings of both, the Mahayana and Hinayana, were committed to collective memory and then eventually to writing. Finally the most secret of Buddha's teachings, the tantras, were also collected, committed to memory and some centuries later put into writing. Parallel to this solidification of the Buddha's teaching Buddhist communities sprang up throughout India. These comprised lay people, who practised as lay householders, and the monastic community, who renounced family and social status in order to engage in a life of celibacy and poverty.

By the time Buddhism reached Tibet, the historical Buddha had faded into the mists of the distant and he functioned mainly as an important shared symbol for the Buddhists. This symbol was understood, interpreted and assimilated differently by the different schools of Buddhism, each of which appropriated the symbol in accordance with his own ideas, presuppositions and practices.

Thervada (Hinayana) Buddhism, for example, developed the idea of a human Buddha—a Buddha endowed with the human attributes of great intellectual abilities, keen insight into the mysteries of life on the one hand and having human failings and limitations on the other hand. The Mahayana school viewed Buddha as a transcendent and cosmic figure. Mahayanists believed that the Buddha appeared among humans as a mere human being but in reality he had surpassed even the great gods of India in his wisdom and power. Like all Buddhists he attained a state of omniscience and was not bound by time or laws of physics and contrary to appearances, he did not really die but instead only appeared to do so. In fact he continues to eternally appear when needed to those who require his help. In Tantrayana or Vajrayana, which grew out of the Mahayana, just as Mahayana grew out of the Hinayana, the emphasis shifted to the use of the body for the development of the mind and the valuable aid which can be given by occult means. Tibetan Buddhists inherited Buddha through stories and so in Tibetan Buddhism he is more important as a powerful symbol than a historical personage. This to a large extent explains the many fantastic mythological episodes attached to his birth, life, personage and teachings.

From the three schools, gradually the Mahayana teachings came to the fore. In the spread of Mahayana many great masters figured but the two most outstanding were Nagarjuna and Asanga, dubbed the 'two great charioteers'. Nagarjuna, Asanga and their followers contributed to the systematization of the awesomely diverse teachings left behind by the Buddha. In their literary compositions they expanded, defended and codified the teachings so that their works became like a key to the treasure chest of Dharma. From their teachings came the two great philosophical schools of Mahayana; Madhyamika or 'Middle Way' and Chittamatra or 'Mind Only'. The Vajrayana, the teaching of the tantras, was transmitted for many generations in secret and it was not until the medieval period that it came to any kind of prominence. From the eighth century AD onwards outstanding masters such as Saraha, Naropa and Virupa contributed to the revitalization of dharma through expounding and practising the tantrik teachings. Such figures are known as the 'siddhas', 'the perfected ones'. They were yogins (practitioners of yoga) who displayed their transcendence of all dualistic preconceptions and fixations through their enlightened and sometimes shocking behaviour.

The emergence of different kinds of schools is indicative not of fission in Buddhism but was a sensible sub-division that presented varied methods of presenting the teachings of the Buddha, for them to appeal to the sensibilities of people, who are essentially different, the world over. As there are so many kinds of practitioners and the dharma is so profound, it would be rather limiting if Buddhism comprised only a single explanation of the path to realization. Thus by the time Buddhism came to an end in India as a religious and social institution in the thirteenth century AD, three waves of teachings had successively flourished – the Hinayana, the Mahayana and the Vajrayana.

10
Sangha—The Monastic Order

In the course of recording the sermons of the Buddha, the Pali Suttas also incidentally record a good deal of information regarding the daily life of the Buddha and his followers. Essentially, the Buddha taught a lifestyle and spiritual discipline whereby others could follow his footsteps and realize for themselves the enlightenment and liberation he had gained under the Bodhi tree.

He established a universal brotherhood—Sangha—of monks, open to all persons of all ranks. Therefore he was the founder of what may be called a kind of universal monastic communism (since Buddhist monks never live alone. A monastic life alone will normally provide the conditions favourable to a spiritual life bent on the highest goal. The monks either lived in communities, or as hermits in solitude. The entire brotherhood of monks and hermits is called the Sangha). Thus Buddha was the first to affirm that true enlightenment was not confined to the Brahmins but open to all members of all castes. In this sense he aimed at abolishing caste, though his followers consisted of a caste of their own by becoming monks, this order of monks was not a hierarchy. He set up no hierarchy except that of strict seniority of membership. A high form of local democracy seems to have prevailed in the order, especially since groups of monks, who were at first supposed to be homeless wanderers by profession and who had to depend on limited supplies of donated food, could grow only so large before they broke up and they moved into a new territory, where they were independent. As a result, the spreading Dharma had no centre which would keep the groups related to each other. It had no ecclesiastical organization under any centralized authority. Buddha appointed no successor. It was not a depository of theological learning. It was a brotherhood, in which all were under certain obligations of celibacy, moral restraint, fasting, poverty, itineration and confession to each other. All were dominated by one idea and pledged to the propagation of one doctrine, that all life in itself was misery and to be got rid of by a long course of discipline, as it is not worth living, whether on earth or in heaven. Buddha believed that the association of monks offered equality of condition to high and low, rich and poor and a haven of refuge to all oppressed by the troubles of life. His order started with first 10, then 50 and later 60 original members but soon it grew to astounding numbers. This carefully regulated monastic brotherhood, which opened its arms to all corners of all ranks and enforced on its members the duty of extending its boundary by constantly rolling forward the Wheel of the True Doctrine, constituting the very essence of Buddhism, without which it never would have been propagated to distant countries.

The reason for the Buddhist community life is inherent in the nature of the Buddha's teaching. His teaching consists of diagnosis and prescription: diagnosis of the human malaise as consisting essentially the disease of individualism, and prescription for its cure as consisting primarily of the erosion of the notion that individuality is something permanent and of great importance. It is in the life of the sangha that the prescription can be most effectively applied; here is the community of being, which comes into existence when the walls of individuality are completely and permanently broken down.

Monasticism has always been a part of the Brahamanical system. According to its most authoritative exponent, Manu's Law Book, man should first be a married householder and then at the end of a long life, abandon his family and become a 'sanayasi' (mendicant). The peculiarity of Buddha's teaching, with regard to monasticism, was that he discouraged solitary asceticism, severe austerities and irrevocable vows, though he enjoined moral restraint in celibate fraternities, conformity to rules of discipline, upright conduct and confession to each other. He designated his monks by the term 'Bhikshu'—'living by alms'—to indicate their poverty.

In the beginning, admission to monk-hood was simple—the Buddha simply said 'come follow me' and discipleship was automatically conferred. But later he commissioned those whom he had admitted, to admit others. The form of admission to the brotherhood is divided into two simple stages marked by two ceremonies. The first—pravrajya—meaning 'going away from home', requires an aspirant to abandon his family and leave home, but with the consent of the parents. This 'novice monk' or 'Navako Bhikku', then cuts off his hair, puts on three ragged yellow garments and recites, before a monk, the Three-Refuge formula:

'I go for refuge to the Buddha (Buddham Sharanam Gachchami)
I go for refuge to the Law (Dhammam Sharnam Gachchami),
I go for refuge to the Order (Sangham Sharnam Gachchami),'

This prayer resembles the 'Gayatri Mantra'—the sacred prayer of the Vedas, consisting of three times eight syllables. The second rite or 'Upsampada' or admission to full monk-hood is a more formal ceremony.

The monks and nuns rose early in the morning, sometimes sitting in meditation before going on their daily alms rounds in a nearby village. They ate only one meal a day, before noon. If the opportunity arose, in the afternoon or evening, they would listen to sermons by the Buddha or his foremost disciples, and then put the teachings into practice by meditating, often long into the night. In addition to monks and nuns, these afternoon and evening sermons were attended by lay followers of the Buddha, interested and sometimes hostile followers of other religious persuasions, and others who were merely curious. Through these sermons by the Buddha and his chief disciples, devotees following this new spiritual path grew steadily in numbers.

Increasingly the Buddha attracted wealthy and even loyal followers who made lavish arrangements to host these sermons. The most colourful of these patrons was Ambapali, reputedly the most sought after courtesan in India. Princes are said to have purchased a night with Ambapali by paving her garden with gold coins. The support of royal and wealthy patrons was essentially the reason for increasing the following of the Buddha. People turned out in thousands to listen to what the most revolutionary teacher of India at that time had to say. But despite his enviable popularity, Buddha and his followers maintained a simple routine wandering the countryside with the barest of possessions, accepting minimal hospitality from their lay followers.

During the monsoon, their wanderings were hampered, due to which the monks and nuns were allowed to take shelter in one place for three months. As more and more of Buddha's followers joined the sangha, specific centers for assembling, during the monsoons, came to be recognized. Initially these were caves and groves of trees, but as the lay following of the Buddha increased in number and wealth, permanent shelters for the monsoon retreats sprang up around the countryside. These were the beginnings of the monasteries, in which it is now customary for Buddhist monks and nuns to live permanently. During the Buddha's times and many generations hence, however, nuns and monks wandered alone or in small groups, the year round, except the monsoons. In addition to the communal retreats of the monsoons, monks and nuns were expected to gather fortnightly for the 'uposatha' days of the new and full moon in order to hear confessions and punish lapses of the discipline. The worst offenders were expelled from the order, but most lapses required only a public apology. As the number of rules governing the sangha increased, the practice of reciting the code of monastic conduct at the end of the 'uposatha' ceremonies was developed. These communal recitations were the beginnings of the oral tradition that endures till the present day. During these monsoon and uposatha gatherings, novices had an opportunity to gain instruction in the teachings of the Buddha by the more experienced followers, who were to become his foremost disciples. These recognized teachings were eventually recorded in collections of scriptures known as the 'Sutta Pitaka', which contains the sermons of the Buddha and his foremost disciples, and the 'Vinaya Pitaka', which contains the rules for the governance of the sangha. At the time of the historical Buddha, however, writing was virtually unknown in India, and so his teachings were preserved through memorization by his disciples. These teachings were transmitted orally for some 500 years, until they were written in Sri lanka, at the beginning of the common era, i.e., at about the time of Jesus. The resulting corpus of literature, known as the Pali canon, is the scriptural basis of Thervada Buddhism.

Originally gatherings, or assemblies were held in the open air; the viharas, in the sense of monasteries, in which they might otherwise have taken place, did not come into existence till a much later period. The word vihara, according to its etymological derivation, denotes a place where the Buddhists assembled; and it is in this sense that this term is used in the sutras, or books considered to contain the words of Sakyamuni Buddha, which always begin thus; 'When Sakya happened to be (viharati sma) at a place'; but later this term was applied to those houses in which the priests met, and where strangers and the ascetics found an asylum. The meaning of the word became more restricted still, and was subsequently given to monasteries only, or to those religious establishments, in which those who once enter them are bound to remain for life. It is impossible to determine exactly the periods during which viharas took the form of meeting houses or later of monasteries. In the Hinayana books on discipline they are mentioned only as an appendix to the chapter on the seats, and they were probably erected later than the temples, the first of which is said to have been built in the period of Upagupta, who lived in the third century BC. The violent attacks of the Brahmins must soon have convinced the Buddhist clergy of the advantages to be derived from association; rules were then drawn for life in community and for subordination, and the beginning of monastic institutions was thus made. In earlier times each vihara had its own administration and its own chief, and was independent of the others; and it was so even in the seventh century, when Hiuen Tsang resided in India; a hierarchy so thoroughly organized as that found in Tibet, was never known in India.

The first organization of the Tibetan clergy dates from King Trisong Detsen. But the development of the present hierarchical system, which was independent of these ancient institutions, dates from the fifteenth century. In 1417, the famous Lama Tsong Khapa founded the Ganden monastery at Lhasa and became its superior; the great authority and reputation he had enjoyed, devolved upon his successors in the abbotship of this monastery, who down to the present day are believed to have been men of particular sanctity. But these abbots were soon superseded in influence by the Dalai Lama and by the Panchen Rinpoche, who are both considered to be of divine origin and are consequently regarded more in the light of gods than of mortal beings.

The next in rank to these sublime lamas are the superiors of several monasteries, of whom some are considered as incarnations, others as common mortals. In either case, head lamas of so high a rank are styled 'Khanpos'. Other persons superior in rank to the common monks are the 'Budzad', the superintendent of the choral songs and music during the divine service, and the 'Gebkoi', who has to maintain discipline and order. These dignitaries are also elected by the monks, and constitute, with the abbot, the council which regulates the affairs of the monastery. Some other dignitaries, which are occasionally found in larger monasteries, are mere posts of honour, having no direct influence upon the administration.

A particular class of lamas consists of astrologers, the Tsikhan, who are allowed to marry and to wear a peculiar fantastic dress. These people are professional fortune tellers, who are officially authorized to conjure and to exercise evil spirits, on behalf of and to the profit of the clergy. Common tricks, such as vomiting fire, swallowing knives, etc. are not openly practised, nor would they be allowed, though in other things these conjurers are permitted to play upon the credulity of the ignorant multitude to any extent, and derive as much profit as they can. The instruments they frequently employ in their incantations are an arrow and a triangle upon which supposed talismanic sentences are inscribed.

The fundamental principle of the monastic lifestyle and discipline was following a middle path, between self-indulgence and self-mortification. The most devoted followers of the Buddha, who became monks and nuns, were expected to abstain entirely from sex, intoxicants, abrasive and harmful conduct. In addition, the Buddha and his following of monks and nuns avoided all luxuries of attire, accommodation and diet, like their teacher; and they moved constantly from place to place lest they became attached even to such rudimentary shelters as a certain cave or tree.

Poverty, celibacy and inoffensiveness were the three essentials of monastic life. A monk possessed almost no private property at all. He was allowed to have his robes, an alms bowl, a needle, a rosary, a razor for shaving the head fortnightly, and a filter which served to remove little animals from his drinking water. Originally, the dress consisted of rags, which were taken from the rubbish heaps in the villages, and which were stitched together and dyed a uniform saffron colour. Later on the cloth for the robes was donated by the faithful. The life of the monk is described as the 'homeless life filled with faith'. The original rigour of the monastic rules seems to have demanded that a monk lived in the forest, in the open or at the foot of a tree. The 'Vinaya' speaks of the dwelling, in convents, sanctuaries, temples, houses and grottos, as of a luxury, permissible but nevertheless full of dangers. Food should be obtained by begging. The Buddhists considered the practice of begging as a breeding ground for many virtues. The monk had no sense of inferiority about this mode of livelihood. He felt that he was not idle by any means, but led a strenuous life, in curbing his desires and developing his meditations. Since generosity is one of the prime virtues, the monks felt that by accepting alms they gave the householder an opportunity for gaining merit.

Celibacy was another cornerstone of the monastic life. Innumerable and meticulous rules hedged in the conduct of a monk towards the women he met on his alms rounds, or whom as nuns, he had to instruct. Unchastity was an offence which automatically led to the expulsion from the order. The monk was warned to be perpetually on his guard, and a short dialogue admirably sums up the attitude of the early Buddhists:

Ananda: 'How should we behave with women?'
Lord: 'Not see them!'
Ananda: 'And if we have to see them?'
Lord: 'Not to speak to them.'
Ananda: 'And if we have to speak to them?'
Lord: 'Keep your thoughts tightly controlled'.

Together with the Buddha and the Dhamma, the Sangha is one of the Three Jewels in Buddhism – one of the three fundamental principles of spiritual life. It is a fellowship of all those who—regardless of lifestyle and background—have dedicated themselves to the attainment of enlightenment. This commitment makes one a member of the Sangha. Among all the seething impulses and emotions, motivations and tendencies, which shape a persons life, this commitment is strong and deep enough for an individual to actively move towards enlightenment.

Buddha created a monastic order, the individuals of which could enter into unity of brotherhood, with all their differences, artificial or otherwise, left behind. Observation made by Buddha in connection with the inauguration of the monastic order:

'Just as, O monks, the great rivers such as the Ganga, Jamuna, Aciravati, Sarabhu and Mahi, when they fall into the ocean, lose their former names and gotras, and are known as the ocean, even so do the four castes—Kshatriyas, Brahmins, Vaisyas and Shudras, when they have gone forth in the doctrine and discipline taught by the Tathagata, from a house to a homeless life, lose their names and gotras and are known as ascetics, sons of the Sakyas'.

11

Buddha—As Legend and History

The story of Buddhism begins with the life and times of its founder, The Enlightened One, but dating of the Buddha's life is a complex problem. On the basis of diverse sources, scholarly estimates of the dates of Buddha's birth and death vary by more than a century. The most common dates given are 563–483 BCE. It is safe and for most purposes sufficient to say that the historical Buddha lived in the decades surrounding 500 BCE.

There is no lack of legendry narratives concerning the Buddha's life, most of them baseless, which the Buddhists enthusiastically relate. While it is easy to place belief in the existence of the historical Buddha, but the Buddha of whom the Buddhist tradition speaks, is too fantastic for belief, being almost without any proof of having existed. This Buddha could not have been a man; his birth, struggles and his death, could by no stretch of imagination been that of a man. However, the existence of a historical personage is strengthened with proofs scattered in various Buddhist texts.

Little is known of the early life of the Buddha, but in his later years as a teacher he stands out as one of the first figures ever to be recorded in history as a real, recognizable human being, rather than a two-dimensional character in a mythologized narration. The early Buddhist scriptures in the Pali script, provides us a glimpse of daily life and historical events and figures in ancient India. On the basis of this material, it is possible to construct a coherent account of the broad outlines of the life of the historical Buddha and an early history of the religion he discovered.

Now 2,000 years prior to the appearance of the Buddha, in approximately, 2500 BCE, is the period of the well flourished Indus Valley civilization. Replete with a written script, elaborate underground drainage and well-planned cities, this civilization, which could have been an authentic source for tracing not only the origins of Buddha and his Buddhism but of all Indian religions, remained buried and forgotten in the debris of 4,000 years. So the backgrounds of Buddhism, based on the archaeological relics of the Indus Valley civilization, are not entirely authentic and believable. A source which is comparatively the most authentic, is the Rig Veda, which lends its content as a source to almost all Indian religions.

The Rig Veda is a scripture containing sacred hymns of the Indo-Europeans who began to arrive in India in approximately 2000 BCE. Like many nomadic peoples, these Indo-Europeans were illiterate, and maintained their sacred traditions and hymns in a memorized, oral tradition. Due to their domination of India, the art of writing disappeared there for some 1,500 years. During this period, not only the Rig Veda, but all of the religious traditions of India had to be maintained and passed on by means of memorized, oral traditions.

Until the rediscovery of the long-forgotten Indus Valley civilization, the Rig Veda was the only source of knowledge about religion in India prior to approximately 1000 BCE. The Rig Veda exhibits few of the prominent characteristics of Hinduism or other Indian religions. Few if any of the major deities of classical Hinduism have convincing counterparts in the Rig Veda, nor is there any real foreshadowing of the almost universal Indian beliefs in an immortal soul, multiple rebirths of the soul determined by one's karma, and spiritual release of the soul (moksha) from rebirth. Instead the hymns of the Rig Veda petition the Vedic deities for material benefits in this life and an afterlife in heaven, characterized as the blissful abode of the ancestors. Alternatively, the Rig Veda mentions a hell of 'blind darkness'. Whether heaven or hell, the Rig Veda envisions only one earthly life and a single afterlife determined primarily on the basis of whether or not one has been scrupulous in performing the proper rituals.

Before the rediscovery of the Indus Valley civilization, on the basis of the Rig Veda alone, it was difficult to explain how belief in souls, rebirth and spiritual release from rebirth came to be so prominent in all of the several religions which developed in India. Discovery of the Indus Valley civilization solved these problems by providing evidence that Indian culture and religion had not developed out of the Vedic religion alone, but rather from a combination of Indo-European and Indus Valley elements. In all its several forms, including Buddhist forms, yoga involves introspective, meditational discipline intended to release the soul from rebirth. Evidence of an Indus Valley deity similar to Shiva suggests that the yogic triad of the belief in souls, rebirth and release derives from indigenous Indian religion rather than from the Rig Veda. All of this evidence suggests that both Buddhism and Hinduism are products of a synthesis of Vedic and yogic religion which occurred during the first millennium BCE. And this indigenous synthesis of harmonizing Vedic and yogic religions is to be found in Hindu scriptures composed between 300 BCE and called the Upanishads.

However, even though the Upanishadic psychological discoveries appear to have influenced the teachings of the historical Buddha, he refused to believe in its concepts regarding the origin of the universe. According to Upanishadic doctrine, the universe is the product of one's own innermost soul. Being a critical and creative participant in a movement to synthesize the ancient traditional world views that vied for the collective heart of India in his time he contributed by offering solutions to conceptual problems which the Upanishadic doctrine created. The historical Buddha refused to speculate upon the origin of the universe, preferring to concentrate on gaining release from rebirth. In this sense, Buddhism belongs to the pre-Vedic, yogic tradition of India. The Buddha, however, denied the existence of the soul, a decidedly non-yogic position. Instead, he incorporated and refined the psychological insights of the Upanishadic sages and offered an analytical theory of the mind which remains remarkably valid even in the modern secular world. Again like the Upanishadic sages, the Buddha held that the attainment of release from rebirth entails realization of the ultimate nature of reality. This position too is more Upanishadic than yogic. The Buddha's notion of ultimate reality, however, was quite contrary to that of the Upanishadic sages, for the Buddha was skeptical regarding any ultimate source of the universe.

The native land of the Buddha can be pointed out on the map of India with some accuracy. Between the Nepalese lower range of the Himalaya and the middle part of the course of the Rapti River, which runs through the north-eastern part of the province of Oudh there stretches a strip of level, fruitful land, broad and well-watered by the numerous streams that issue from the Himalayas. Here lay the not very extensive territory over which the Sakyas claimed supremacy and dominion. On the east the Rohini separated their lands from their neighbours; to this day this stream has preserved the name which it bore more than 2,000 years ago. On the west and the south the rule of the Sakyas extended quite up to the Rapti.

Of Gautama's childhood and early youth next to nothing is known from earlier texts. But there are contained descriptions in them, of the wonders which attended his birth, and the precocity of the young Gautama. 'He was not born as ordinary men are; he had no earthly father; he descended of his own accord into his mother's womb from his throne in heaven; and he gave unmistakable signs, immediately after his birth, of his high character and of his future greatness. Earth and heaven at his birth united to pay him homage, the very trees bent of their own accord over his mother, and the angels and archangels were present with their help. His mother was the best and the purest of the daughters of men. And his father was of royal lineage, a king of wealth and power. It was a pious task to make his abnegation and his condescension greater by the comparison between the splendour of the position he was to abandon, and the poverty in which he afterwards lived. And in countries distant from Kapilvastu, the inconsistencies between such glowing accounts, and the very names they contain, passed unnoticed by credulous hearers.' (Rhys Davis)

Such legends are indeed of the greatest possible historical value from the comparative point of view. Similar legends are related of all the founders of the great religions, and even of the more famous kings and conquerors in the ancient world.

In approximately 250 BCE, the Indian emperor Ashoka erected an inscribed granite pillar at the birthplace of the Buddha, a village called Lumbini in what is today southern Nepal. Unfortunately, Ashoka's inscription does not specify how many years had passed since the Buddha's birth. As a result, the Buddha's birthplace is more certain than his birth date. The biography of Buddha has not come down to us from ancient times, from the age of the Pali texts, and, we can safely say no such biography was in existence then. The idea of a biography was unknown to the people in those times. For the earliest Buddhists it was the word of the Buddha rather than the life of the Buddha, which seems to have been of paramount importance. It was the discourses which were remembered, rehearsed at his death, and carefully preserved and transmitted in the community of his followers. His life story was not in itself a matter of such intrinsic interest apparently, since the canon of scripture of the Theravadin School, which is representative of early or 'primitive Buddhism', contains no continuous narrative of his life. It was not until later, in Buddhist history, that full length biographies of the Buddha were produced.

We know about Buddha's native country and about the family from which he came. We know about his parents, the early death of his mother, and about her sister, who brought him up. Buddhist legends also universally portray the Buddha's father Suddhodhana was a mighty ruler of a busy town Kapilvastu, on the north-west to south-east trade route which ran along the foot of the Himalayan Mountains, amid the thick forests at the extreme edge of the Gangetic plain. It lay towards north of modern day Varanasi, and a few miles within the border of what is now Nepal. The Buddha belonged to the clan of the Gautamas, and it is by this name that he is often known, though he was, christened Siddharta. The names by which he is most commonly designated—Sakya-muni and Buddha, are titles which he acquired after enlightenment. The kingdom of the Sakyas was one of those aristocratic governments, a number of which had maintained themselves on the outskirts of the greater Indian monarchies. Of these greater monarchies there stood in close proximity to the Sakyas, the powerful kingdom of Kosala, adjoining it on the south and west. The Sakyas looked upon themselves as Kosalas, and the kings of the Kosala claimed certain rights over them; later they are said to have brought the Sakya-land wholly within their power and to have exterminated the ruling family. But even though the Sakyas occupied an insignificant respect of military and political power among their neighbours, the haughty spirit which prevailed in their ancient family was characteristic of the Sakya line. Of the wealth of the Sakyas also it is said, 'A family blessed with prosperity and great opulence'.

A widespread tradition represents Buddha as having been a king's son. At the head of this aristocratic community there must certainly have been one leading man appointed with the title of the king. But the idea that Buddha's father enjoyed this royal dignity is quite foreign to the oldest forms in which the traditions regarding the family are presented to us: rather we have nothing more or less to contemplate in Suddhodhana than one of the great and wealthy landowners of the Sakya race, whom later legends first transformed into the 'great king suddhodhana'. Scarcely anything about Buddha's childhood is known. A stepmother, Prajapati, and a stepsister have been mentioned, while his own mother died within a week of giving birth to him.

During pregnancy, his mother, the beautiful queen Maya, is said to have received auspicious omens heralding the exalted status of the child she bore, most notably a dream of a white elephant entering her abdomen when the prince was conceived. The birth is said to have occurred not in the royal palace at Kapilvastu, but in a nearby park at Lumbini, while Queen Maya was on a pleasure outing. This detail may well be a historical fact, but accounts of the birth itself can scarcely be accepted as history. We know a number of other facts which extend over the several parts of his life. It would be quite inconceivable even in India, if the church which called itself by the name of the son of the Sakya house had, within a century after his death, ceased to preserve, even though veiled in legend, a correct memory of the most important names of the persons around the Buddha, and of certain leading public events in his life. Even the name of Buddha's native town Kapilvastu is a subject of suspicion—Kapilvastu, was the abode of the Kapila, the mythical philosopher Kapila, the founder of the Sakya school. The very existence of this town itself is not guaranteed by any of the available evidence. The Chinese pilgrims, who travelled in India in the fifth and seventh centuries after Christ, claimed that they saw the ruins of the town. But it is doubtful whether ruins indicate the town to which they belong. However, the strongest confirmation of the claims of the Chinese pilgrims, lies in the fact that, on the one hand, the occasional direct statements and indirect hints of the sacred Pali works regarding the site of the town, and, on the other hand, the route of the pilgrims who looked for it, if both are to be traced on the map of India, coincide exactly. In addition to this, at the place where, according to this evidence, Buddha's home must have been, there is a small stream which, even in the present day, bears the same name (Rohini) as was borne by a stream in the territory of the Sakyas often mentioned in the Buddhist traditions.

Among the opulent and gentle youth of that age, it was indispensable to the comfort of a style of life in keeping with their dignity, to have three palaces, which were constructed to be occupied by turns corresponding to the changes of winter, summer and rains. Tradition states that the coming Buddha passed his early years in three such palaces, leading a life seeped in luxuries. It is easily comprehensible how, in the oppressive monotony of idle ease and satiated enjoyment, a restless and introspective nature as that of the Buddha, would have easily broken loose, being unable to find satisfaction in an empty world of transitory pleasure. It would be difficult to speculate the nature of the thoughts that must have pervaded the mind of the young Gautama, that led him to leave home and lead a life devoid of even the basic amenities.

However, from early texts, this much then is clear that Gautama was born in a family belonging to the highest ruling caste of the small Aryan community centred at Kapilvastu in Kosala. The later accounts would lead to an inference that the Sakya domain was a rich and extensive country, though there is nothing in the older books to confirm this. Indeed, from the references to the adjoining state, it would seem to have been a small territory; not much more than 1500sq.mi. in extent. His people were agriculturists and, no doubt, the economic position even of the principal families among them was of a very simple kind. All the marvellous details of the wealth and glory of the royal palace, in which he lived in oriental luxury, could in all probability have been due to the natural desire to magnify the splendour of the position he renounced, when for the sake of others he came out as a mendicant.

In his twenty ninth year Gautama abandoned his home, wife and infant son and went forth into the world to become a homeless wanderer, and to spend his life, first in thinking out for himself the deepest problems of experience, and then in spreading abroad to others the good tidings of the salvation which he deemed himself to have discovered. It may seem quite an unnecessary step on the part of the Buddha to leave his house in order to find answers to his yearnings. But during those days, to work in one's study for the regeneration of mankind was almost impossible. There were no written books through which to communicate with the outside world. On the other hand the necessities were much fewer and much simpler. During those times, to retire into the woods and to devote one's self to the higher life was not only practicable, but was even not uncommon. In the law books, by which the lives of the Brahmins were regulated, it is considered so much a matter of course that a man should retire from the world and that the life of the good Brahmin is divided into three stages. During the first stage he is to acquire education and knowledge under the tutelege of an accomplished master, during the second stage he is to marry, rear a family and perform all the religious rites and sacrifices, and the household duties of a good Brahmin – and during the third of it he is to leave his home and retire, with or without his wife, into the forest, and live as a recluse, a life of meditation. It was a matter of common belief at that time, that by the practice of austere self-mortification, a man could compel the gods to manifest themselves to him and reveal the truth; and also that the suppression of bodily feeling would in itself open out the way to a greater vigour of the mind and to extraordinary insight.

In this period occurred what is arguably the most profound and widespread intellectual and spiritual transformation the world has ever seen. In China, Confucius and Lao Tzu were formulating the principles of Confuscianism and Taoism, systems of ethics and religion which would guide nearly one quarter of the human race into the present century. Zoroaster (founder of Zoroastrianism) in Persia and a few decades later Socrates in Greece were laying the ideological foundations of the empires that dominated the classical history of the western world, the Persian, the Greek and the Roman. Following the Babylonian exile of the Jews, Jeremiah and Second Isaiah, author of most of the book of Isaiah in the Hebrew Bible, were formulating the principles of universal monotheism, the philosophical basis of Judaism, Christianity and Islam. In India, at the time of the Buddha, composition of the principle

Upanishads (between 800 and 300 BCE), the first scriptures of classical Hinduism, was in mid-course. The Pali books give us an exceedingly concrete picture of the movements of the religious world of India at the period in which Buddha, if he really lived, must have played a part in it; we possess the most minute details of all the holy men who, sometimes standing alone and sometimes surrounded by communities of adherents, with and without organization, some in more profound and some in more shallow terms, preached to the people salvation and deliverance. Six great teachers are mentioned, among others, as contemporaries of Buddha – the heads of six sects holding other faiths. The coming of such a sudden turning-point in Buddha's inner life corresponds much too closely with what in all times similar natures have actually experienced under similar conditions, for us not to be inclined to believe in such an occurrence. In the most widely different periods of history the notion of a revolution or change of the whole man perfecting himself in one moment meets us in many forms: a day and an hour it seems must be possible to determine, in which the unsaved and unenlightened becomes a saved and enlightened man: and if men look and hope for such a sudden break through of the soul to the light, it is highly possible for them to realize it. Natures endowed with the most versatile powers of imagination, are especially susceptible to such experiences. Some Buddhist texts, in recreating the picture of the times of the Buddha, narrate about the belief in a sudden illumination of the soul and about the fact of an internal emancipation perfecting itself in one moment, and this seemed to be a universally prevalent belief. Experiencing the moment of illumination, which ultimately led to emancipation, was an ambition commonly harboured by the youth of Buddha's day. This ambition was generated and strengthened by the spiritual masters of the day, who promised their followers that if they trod the right path, 'after a short time, that for which noble youths leave their homes and lead a pilgrim life, the highest achievement of religious effort, would be vouchsafed to him, that he would yet in this life apprehend the truth itself, and see it face to face'. This visionary grasp of truth was pursued by mortification by some and by abstraction of the mind by others, pushing themselves to the farthest limit through long protracted retention of the body in fixed postures, all waiting for the moment in which the attainment of their aim would be clearly realized by them with absolute certainty. When any one came to regard his natural state as impermanent and dark, that to which he aspired, and which he, therefore, expected finally to actually realize, could not but appear to him to be a condition of purer internal illumination and self-knowledge, and with this condition of pure internal illumination was combined the consciousness of his own power to look, by visionary intuition, through the whole concatenation of the universe.

Considering the society of those times, it is believable for us that harbouring of such views and ambitions among the religious inquirers at Buddha's time was only natural. Whosoever abandoned his home to become a mendicant did so with an eye on the coveted fruit of enlightenment. A similar expectation would then have so consumed Buddha that he traded a life of luxury for a life of derivation.

In the sixth century BC there must have happened in India, something very important – some very great social, moral, political and religious changes – that brought about the birth of the Buddha. To understand the social scene that initiated the birth of the Enlightened One, we must go back in time, at least a 1,000 years before Buddha's birth—the time of the Aryan advent and settling into India. In the course of 15 centuries, from the time of Aryan advent to the birth of the Buddha, the Aryans would have undoubtedly witnessed numerous social, moral, political and religious changes. The most sublime of these changes definitely occurred in their religion, which developed and grew into the grandest of all religions that Buddha was to preach 15 centuries later. The Aryans entered the land of the five rivers, tending their sheep and cattle and singing their sweet songs of nature;

'*Risen in majestic blaze,*
lo! the universe's eye.
Vast and wonderous best of rays,
shineth brightly in the sky.'

The Aryans were resourceful, intelligent and energetic; they improved themselves in every department—in agriculture, architecture, science, literature and philosophy. They steadily grew powerful, wealthy and mighty.

But where wealth has joys and comforts on one side, it has misery and dissension written on its other side. Even as the Aryans grew in wealth, internal dissensions marred their lives. The fighting class became prominent and began lording over the others. They protected the country, shed their blood to protect all the others, they only considered it logical for them to be the rulers. The warriors, though they lorded over all, were perforce bound by reverence to honour the custodians of their religious affairs, endowed by knowledge and learning. Slowly society settled into a sub-division of four broad categories or castes—the warriors or Kshatriyas, the priests or Brahmins, the agriculturists and traders or Vaisyas and lastly the conquered black slaves or the shudras. With the passage of time, this sub-division of society into castes became an established system, in which the 'higher' castes mistreated and exploited the 'lower' castes. Also, the Brahmins, in sole charge of religious activities and possession of scriptural learning, forced upon the ignorant populace a religion rife with meaningless rituals and superstitions. There was a total disintegration of cohesion in the country of the Aryan settlers. The Indians, during the sixth century BC pinned under the pressure of spiritual and worldly servitude and waited for a reliever who appeared to them in the person of the Buddha.

The pantheism of the Brahmanical religion gave incidence to two doctrines—emanation and transmigration. All things have emanated from Brahma; all must return to him again. But this absorption, into the divine, is regulated. Those who have served and known Brahma, will be absorbed into him at death; those who have not done so must pass through purgatory proportioned to their guilt. All the sorrows that afflict a man here must trace to the guilt he had contracted in his former lives. And only by passing through an almost endless succession of punishments and births and revolting experiences could man win back the way to a welcome extinction in Brahma. Nothing could tell more powerfully on the popular imagination.

Two conclusive beliefs emerged, and took root, from this Brahmanical religion: one this, that the Brahmins, without whom no sacrifice could be performed, and no deliverance from the alarming prospect effected, gained absolute supremacy, and religion in consequence became more and more a matter of ceremony, less and less a matter of morality. Secondly, as in a pantheistic system there can be no absolute immortality of individuals, and as all persons must eventually be absorbed in the impersonal existence, the rewards and punishments of men must have a limit. Reward as well as punishment must terminate. But so long as men do good, they deserve reward, as they deserve punishment when they do evil. Works of all kinds, therefore, must be got rid of. Man's highest state is the state of contemplative abstraction, in which nothing is done. Salvation, that is to say, is to be obtained by priestly rites and transcendental knowledge.

Whatever profound thoughts lay about the roots of Brahmanism, and however suitable to the Hindu mind it may originally have been, there can be no question that it held the people of India, as it still holds them, in a bondage, at once tyrannical and degrading. It was against the demoralizing ritualism and the despotic nature of this religion that the revolt at last came in the form of Buddhism.

Buddha overthrew the entire system of ritualistic practice, discarded the classification of men into castes and every type of mortification for attainment of deliverance:

'Neither the fish, flesh nor the fasts, neither going naked nor tonsure, neither the braid of hair nor decoration, nor the rough hides nor the veneration of the fire, nor the practice of penance, nor the hymns nor the offerings, nor the sacrifice, purify men who have not conquered doubt.'

'No one becomes a Brahmin through the braid of hair, through his family, through his birth. He who possesses honesty and veracity, he is blessed, he is a Brahmin.'

'What is the use of your braided hair, O you fool, what is the use of garments of goat-skin? Your inner is impure, you purify the exterior.'

'I call nobody a Brahmin on account of his birth or on account of his mother. He may be even talking proudly and he may be even rich. The poor, who is free from lusts him I call a Brahmin.'

He also expressed his objections to the means which the Brahmins employed to gain their end: 'if abstention from sufficient food is meritorious, the wild beasts, who are content with grass, ought to abound in merit; and the man who now suffers hardships ought, as a necessary consequence, to enjoy future happiness.' And he exploded, as summarily, the sacrificial rites performed by the Brahmins, 'How can the system, which requires the infliction of misery on others be called a religious system? To seek a good by doing an evil is surely no safe plan. If a man, in worshipping the gods, sacrifices a sheep, and so does well, why should he not kill his child and so do better?' To these conjectures of his, the Brahmins had little to reply.

Buddha sharply invalidated the unjust claims of the nobility like those of the Brahmins and every difference of caste disappeared for him when it did not concern itself with earthly objects but when it dealt with the otherworldly. But this was not his notion, not anything new. The same opinion was represented by Kapila, the founder of the Samakhya philosophy. Badarayana, the founder of the Vendata, the orthodox Brahmanical system taught that the three higher castes alone are entitled to absolution. In contrast to this, the Samakhya taught, that all men without any difference of position can be absolved and that everyone who has acquired right knowledge can also lead others to right knowledge and thereby be absolved. The Vedanta taught that sacrifice and other pious works lead to absolution and thus it makes external piety also forcibly obligatory for one struggling for salvation. On the other hand, the Samakhya expressly dissuaded the offering of sacrifices and taught that only good work does not lead to the attainment of right knowledge but obstructs it. It lays no stress at all on morality. And this is the great difference between it and Buddhism. As a contrast to it, Buddha laid great emphasis on a strict moral life.

It was mainly opposition to the Brahmanical sacrificial and social system which the Buddha shared with other contemporary Indian teachers, or 'Shramans'. The term shraman refers to non-Brahmins but among these 'non-conformist' mendicant philosophers there were some Brahmins by birth who also rejected the authority of the Vedic scriptures and the caste system of their day. Each shraman with his disciples constituted a sect and between them these sects covered a variety of views, or philosophical positions, from materialism to mysticism. There seems, however, to have been an earlier stage, when there was practically no sectarian organization, but only a large number of individual ascetic, homeless wanderers, known in a broad sense as 'Ajivakas'. This later became the name of a particular sect, but a little before the time of the Buddha, the term was applied to all those who had adopted the 'ajiva', or 'special way of life which was an alternative to ordinary trade'. This alternative way of life was embraced, says A.K. Warder, 'by many who wished to escape the need to work, or the responsibility of family life, not to speak of conscription, forced labour or slavery, and was a carefree existence very different from the life of strenuous asceticism, complicated discipline, and intensive study required of members of most of the organized sects afterwards'. This opting out of the social and economic life of the time seems to have been the one feature common to men of otherwise widely varying viewpoints, all of whom, however, were skeptical of the accepted religious philosophy of the Brahmins. By the time of the Buddha, wandering, mendicant ascetics in considerable numbers were a familiar feature of the social scene. Evidently then, the Buddha belongs to the company of the shramans, the non-Brahmin teachers, who were critical of the Brahmanical sacrificial system and who rejected the religious and social claims of the Brahmins. He was a historical sage and teacher, who worked out his own peace by his own methods of meditation.

12
Buddhist Thought and Its Relevance

Cicero's interpretation of the word 'religion' is: a repetition of prayers and incantations. Another derivation makes its original sense, that of attachment, of a continual binding (most probably to the gods). The third derivation explains the word as a law abiding, scrupulously conscientious frame of mind, with law in the early days not meaning legislation but custom, established precedent and a sense of duty to the established order of things. Quoting T.W. Rhys Davis (*Buddhism: Its History and Literature*) 'it is evident that man's definitions of religion will be precisely as numerous, as different and as accurate as their own belief'.

The word religion has no fixed meaning. Having passed through many stages, it has been subject to numerous changes and adaptations through each stage. Religion initially came to be identified with beliefs, rituals, ceremonies, prayers and sacrifices. This led to the stage of a creator, or, God, followed by belief in the soul, which is eternal and unanswerable to god.

The Tibetan language does not even have a term with the same associations as the English word 'religion'. The closest is the word 'Cho' (chos), which is the Tibetan translation of the Sanskrit word 'Dharma' (dhamma in Pali). Buddhism is an entirely a Western coinage. To its followers it is known as 'Dharma', Dharma meaning 'The Truth', in the sense of the ultimate reality of things – the true nature of existence. It is 'truth', an ideal to be sought and realized by each human being. It also means 'the truth' in the sense of a teaching or practice, which helps the individual to develop, to realize for himself a greater degree of truth.

Buddha called Dharma fundamentally different from what was called religion. The word Dharma means 'that which holds'. Any elevated action of body, speech or mind is regarded as Dharma because through such an action one is protected or 'held back' from all sorts of disasters. Dharma simply means the Law. One cannot worship it. This is the great contribution of Buddha to the world: religion in his understanding is Law; one has to live it, live according to it, as this Law is the norm of the universe. Living against it will bring misery and living it will lead to bliss. Buddhism, or more accurately Dharma, is the means to enlightenment. The Buddha himself compares it to a raft, which after being fashioned out of grass, sticks, branches and leaves, serves to cross over great stretches of water and is then abandoned, so the Dharma, by means of which we ferry over the waters of birth and death to the shore of Nirvana (enlightenment), is not something to be taken with us but something to be left behind. Implying it is only a means to an end, its function being purely instrumental and therefore its value only relative.

The pragmatism of the Dharma has been emphasized by the Buddha to his foster mother and aunt, Mahapajapati Gautami, who had asked him to give her a percept hearing which she might dwell 'alone, solitary, ardent and resolved'. The Buddha replies thus: 'Of whatever teachings, thou canst assure thyself thus: 'These doctrines conduce to dispassion, to passions; to detachment, not to bondage; to decrease of (worldly) gains, not to an increase of them; to frugality, not to covetousness; to content and no to discontent; to solitude, not company; to energy, not sluggishness; to delight in good, not delight in evil'; of such teachings thou mayest with certainty affirm, Gautami, 'This is the Dharma'.

The Dharma specifies that you are your own master and thus self-examination is the only way to the realization of existence. The Buddhist theory of self-responsibility entails self-examination and self-control in consideration of both one's own and other's interests. The central idea of Buddhism is, bringing about a radical change in human nature, which can come through self-examination. This change is a transformation of man himself, for, man is not a complete final being. He is a being who can transform himself and thereby transform the society and the psychological environment, bringing about peace for himself, peace for the society and peace for the world.

Peace and happiness are the highest ideals sought by all existence and every endeavour of humankind is directed towards the attainment of these two ideals. Buddhism sees peace (santi) and happiness (sukha) as synonymous: an unhappy person cannot find peace and there can be no peace without happiness; in the Buddha's words: 'there is no higher happiness than peace'. When the Buddha realized that Kapila, an ancient Indian philosopher and sage, had talked much about suffering without showing the way to remove it, he left the ashrama of Alarkalam, pondered over the problem and eventually found a right solution for the removal of human misery. That is why the Buddha is regarded as the 'margdata', the way finder. After his enlightenment, he travelled on foot from village to village, in order to help the suffering people and to guide those who indulged in sensuous pleasures and other worldly attractions. He showed the way to live with peace, honesty and equality in society.

Peace as implied by the Buddha is not a condition of unstable political equilibrium but rather a state of mind, purified from all feelings of antagonism and thoroughly permeated by that impersonal and universal love which Buddhists call 'maitri'. If peace, which is a form of love, is not universal, it is not universal at all. The conclusion of a private peace between two or more nations, to the exclusion of the remainder, is in reality impossible. Should such a 'peace' in any way threaten the security of any other state, even its observance would be no higher a moral plane than the honesty that is popularly supposed to exist among thieves.

Even the most industrious research has been unable to dig out from the 2,500 years of Buddhist history, during which time it spread over more than the quarter of the land surface of the globe, as many as ten incidents of violence. Not a single page of Buddhist history has ever been lurid with the light of inquisitorial fires, or darkened with the smoke of heretic or heathen cities. Buddhism wields only one sword, the sword of peace, and recognizes only one enemy – ignorance. Tibet, before the introduction of Buddhism was the greatest military power in Asia. The early history of Burma, Siam (Thailand) and Kampuchea (Cambodia), shows that the people of these countries originally had an aggressive, war like disposition. The Mongol hordes overran, not only whole of central Asia, but also India, China, Persia and Afghanistan. The martial spirit of Japan is well-known too. Apart from India and China, the nations of Asia were originally no less pugnacious and predatory, than those of Europe. Their subsequent peacefulness was due very largely to the influence of the pacific teachings of Buddhism. It could hardly have pacified turbulent and war like nations by preaching to them a god of battles. It may therefore be concluded that the association between Buddhism and peace is not fortuitous but inevitable. Buddhism has been in the past, is at present and will continue to be active in the establishment of universal peace.

Dr. Radhakrishnan (the 2nd President of India) has reminded us of the Buddhist ideals for individual and international peace: "The Buddha aimed at the development of a new type of free man, free from prejudice, intent on working out his own future, with reliance on one's self, 'attadipa'. His humanism crossed racial and national barriers. Yet the chaotic condition of world affairs reflects the chaos in men's souls. History has become universal in spirit. Its subject matter is neither Europe, nor Asia, neither east nor west, but humanity in all lands and ages. In spite of political divisions, the world is one, whether we like it or not. The fortunes of everyone are linked up with those of others. But we are suffering from an exhaustion of spirit, an increase of egoism, individual and collective, which seem to make the ideal of the world society too difficult to desire. What we need today is a spiritual view of the universe...we must recover the lost ideal of spiritual freedom. If we wish to achieve peace, we must maintain the inner harmony, that poise of the soul, which are the essential elements of peace."

The whole world is at present panic-stricken and on the verge of calamities. The big powers are not secured as far as their existence is concerned. They are threatened to death by their self-made strategy resulting in an apprehension of total devastation. This state of the world is not something new, history of humanity from the very beginning to this day records great numbers of wars. Since the sacred and patriotic, just and courageous act of war has been approved as a fundamental condition for human survival, the history of humanity has become a history of war. War is not an act of barbarians, it is carried out by the so-called most modern, civilized men. Nations which boast of possessing the most up to date civilizations in the world, lavishly waste a certain percentage of their total production in their schemes of war, in the name of national defence expenditure.

However, strife never was and will never be a way out. The answer is non-violence versus violence, the heart and mind versus weaponry. The independence of India was attained owing to Gandhi's complete relinquishment of his living. He lived in a mud hut, and accomplished that revolution from within such life. When humanity stops claiming food as their priority, but instead seeks for the righteous path, the nuclear weapons would be of no use. On the contrary, because it is claimed that people must eat, nuclear weapons start to mean something. The scientific civilization has lost sight of moral values in the purpose of human existence. It is unable to see spiritual dignity in man, and considers that the principle of human survival lies merely in attainment of victory in competition.

War has been aggravated and nuclear weapons developed on the basic faith in the theory that the 'stronger is the victor and the weaker, the loser'. Modern scientific civilization, which originated in Europe in the sixteenth century, developed recklessly and out of control. As a result, it is at the height of its fury and poses the threat of human annihilation and destruction of the natural environment.

According to the theory of evolution, the rule on which our society is based is explained as "the law of the jungle", the struggle for existence. Snakes must catch and eat frogs to live. Tigers must catch deer and eat them to live. No one can prohibit them from doing so. Human beings have also learned to take the lives of others to protect their own lives. The killing and eating of man might be tolerated if there is no other way for humans to survive. However, man conducts war not for the sake of eating soldiers or those whom he kills, but merely for the sake of killing. The way of life of the present humanity is a misfortune.

The Buddha was a historical sage who worked out his own 'peace' by his own efforts and methods of spiritual 'sadhna', or meditation. The Buddha's Nirvana (enlightenment) was that very state of peace described by his predecessors. The Buddha after his enlightenment wanted to share the bliss of peace with all beings subject to suffering and sorrow. So his universal prayer was: "Sabbe satta sukhita hontu", may all beings be happy. His command to his monk disciples was to move round the world, "for good of the many, for happiness of the many", "Bahujana hitaya, bahujana sukhaya". The Buddhist ideal, since the time of the Buddha, is being materialized with this dictum 'good and happiness'. The doctrine of the Buddha, the aim for happiness and peace for an individual and for all, is being re-valued, reconsidered and realized in a new perspective since the later part of the last century of the Christian era.

In addition to seeking and spreading peace and happiness, another fundamental principle of Buddhist ethics is that all men should develop an attitude of compassion. True wisdom consists not in metaphysical sophistication, but in practical knowledge, which is expressed in the attitude of compassion or love of one's neighbours – highly esteemed in Buddhism. Compassion is 'metta' in Pali and 'maitri' in Sanskrit, both words literally meaning 'true friendliness'. Loving kindness and compassion are two cornerstones on which the whole edifice of Buddhism stands. Destruction or injury of any kind of life is strictly forbidden. Buddha said, "Do not harm others. Just as you feel affection on seeing a dearly beloved person, so should you extend loving kindness to all creatures." When we look around we see large scale violence, killings, famines, hunger and frustrations. We have knowledge without understanding; criticism without appreciation; reasoning without logic; friendship without sincerity and relationship without commitment. In this social and emotional turmoil love is the only sanction of life. There is a saying in the 'Tripitaka', a Buddhist text, "As a mother even at the risk of her own life watches over her own child, so let everyone cultivate a boundless compassion towards all beings".

His holiness the 14th Dalai Lama, believes that non-violent resistance is the only path. His ideas on compassion and non-violence are revered and emulated the world over: "When we take into account a larger perspective, the fact that all wish to gain happiness and avoid suffering, and keep in mind our relative unimportance in relation to countless others, we can conclude that it is worthwhile to share our possessions with others. When you train in this sort of outlook, a true sense of compassion, a true sense of love and respect for others, becomes possible. Individual happiness ceases to be a conscious self-seeking effort; it becomes an automatic and far superior by-product of the whole loving and serving others. Compassion karuna, is the wish to help others find enlightenment in suffering. Buddha taught compassion as the highest virtue.

However, compassion, or tolerance does not mean that you accept your defeat or you let wrong doing triumph. It does not mean that you may not take a strong counter measure in order to stop that which is wrong. Meanwhile, deep down, you should not lose your compassion.

Individuals can make a difference in society. To develop compassion is not just from a religious point of view but from a humanitarian one as well. The practice of compassion is not just a symptom of unrealistic idealism, but the most effective way to pursue the best interest of others as well as own. The more we as nations or as individuals depend upon others, the more it is in our own best interest to ensure their well-being. Some people seem to think that compassion is just a passive emotional response instead of rational stimulus to action. To experience genuine compassion is to develop a feeling of closeness to others, combined with a sense of responsibility for their welfare. True compassion develops when we accept that other people are just like ourselves in wanting happiness and not suffering, and that they have every right to pursue these" (Taken from H.H. Dalai Lama's book *A Human Approach to World Peace*).

His Holiness the Dalai Lama further asserts, on the matter of compassion and non-violence, which form the basic tenets of Buddhism:

"True compassion is universal in scope it is accompanied by a feeling of responsibility. To act altruistically, concerned only for the welfare of others with no selfish or ulterior motives, is to affirm a sense of universal responsibility. For a Buddhist monk, the cultivation of compassion is an important part of my daily practice. One aspect involves merely sitting quietly in my room, meditating. That can be very good and very comfortable, but the true aim of cultivating compassion is to develop the courage to think of others and to do something for them. It is easier to meditate than to actually do something for others.

But merely to meditate on compassion is to take passive option. Our meditation should form the basis of action, for seizing the opportunity to do something. The meditator's motivation, his sense of universal responsibility, should be expressed in deeds....

One of the most powerful emotions disturbing our mental tranquility is hatred. The antidote is compassion. We should not think of compassion as being only the preserve of the sacred and the religious. It is one of our basic human qualities. Human nature is essentially loving and gentle. Human beings are innately non-aggressive, despite the apparent prevalence of anger and hatred in the world. From the moment of our birth we require love and affection. This is true of us all, right up to the day we die..."

Compassion in Buddhism also has an ecological value; ecological value is that of responsibility, which exceeds one's own ego. This responsibility is towards the entire environment, for the whole planet, for other human beings, for other living beings, for the cosmos at large. A Buddhist deeply believes in the interconnectedness of all things, it would be impossible for such a one to shrug off one's responsibility for the well-being of other forms of life. Thus according to Buddhist ethic, compassion is also a form of responsibility, and conversely, genuine responsibility for the well-being of others must express itself, at times through compassion.

The Buddhist attitude towards morality is in great contrast to that of other world religions. Buddhism is a philosophy of optimism based on 'bahujana hitaya' (well-being of all), 'bahujana sukhaya' (happiness of all). The highest good is to be found not in the domination of one race, religion or nationality over another, but in a co-operative commonwealth, in which the welfare of all beings is ensured. Most of the world religions, however, base their moral principles on tribal ethics; their rules are primarily concerned with the survival, cohesion and prosperity of the tribe or nation. Laws such as these were framed to meet specific needs and circumstances and not invariably rules to be adopted and observed by all men in all ages. Some of these laws have survived into highly developed cultures in the form of caste-rules, or, indirectly in the direction of racial antagonism. Even today we cannot find any racial or national group that is entirely free from these deep-rooted prejudices.

In Buddhism however, the approach to morality is entirely different. Buddhism did not begin as a tribal religion; it was universal in character from its initiation onwards. The Buddha did not assume the role of a law-giver, and consequently Buddhism did not develop along legalistic lines. It did not enforce a set code of laws governing marriage, the transmission of property, the punishment of criminals and other secular matters. It is concerned with each man's individual spiritual welfare. The ethical imperatives of theistic religions express man's duty towards god or nation through his duty towards his fellow-men. But Buddhism does not acknowledge any 'Supreme Being' as creator of the universe; it does not lay down any commandments respecting obligations to unseen powers. Neither does it have any divine forgiveness for sins. In Buddhism, the individual's duty towards others expresses his duty towards himself; that is to cleanse himself of the mental defilements of greed, hatred and delusion. Thus Buddhist morality is neither the mandate of a supreme being whose existence is called into question, nor is it solely the invention of human mind.

Buddhism believes life to be nothing but suffering and subsequently has a well-defined path, which helps realize and weed out the foundations of this universal suffering. According to the Buddhist meditation theory, the basic causes of suffering are cognitive in origin. We mentally create a vision of reality, but because of ignorance this vision is skewed and does not reflect things as they are. Some of our wrong ideas are harmless but others lead to the creation of negative mental states, such as ignorance, desire and hatred. One of the most dangerous of these wrong ideas, is the false notion of the self, which Buddhist meditation theory contends is innately present in all human beings. On a very basic level, every person believes in a self or soul that is uncreated, immortal, unchanging and permanent. Contrary to some other religious systems, Buddhism denies the existence of such an entity and contends that in order to attain liberation one must eliminate the false idea of a self or soul. But if the concept is common to all human beings, where do we get it from? And if it a false concept, why is it so universally accepted? The answer, Buddhist texts suggest is that, although there is a basis for this idea of the self, the imputation is still a false one. The basis for the imputation of the self is the collection of elements that constitute the psycho-physical personality, which Buddhism divides into five 'aggregates'—form, feelings, discriminations, compositional factors and consciousness.

These are the constituents of all impermanent phenomena and are the basis on which we impute the notions of 'I' and 'mine'. Taken together, they are the constituents of the individual, but we mistakenly impute something more, an essence, a self or soul. When one analyzes this concept to locate its basis, however, all that one finds are these five aggregates, none of which can constitute a self because they are constantly changing, whereas the self that sentient beings imagine is self-sufficient and enduring.

Taken together, these five aggregates constitute the sum total of the psycho-physical personality, and Buddhist teachers claim that the totality of an individual is included within this group. Ordinary beings, however, impute something more, an enduring, uncreated self that exists apart from and independently of the aggregates, but this is nothing more than a label imputed to these constantly changing factors. This mistaken notion leads to grasping and attachment, which in turn result in suffering, and so the mistaken belief in the self is said to be one of the most powerful factors that keep ordinary beings enmeshed in cyclic existence. The Dalai Lama explains about the nature of this wrongly believed in 'self' thus: "Let us illustrate this with the example of a rosary, which has 108 beads. The whole, the one rosary, has 108 beads as its parts. The parts and the whole are [conventionally] different; yet, when the parts are eliminated, a rosary cannot be found. Because the rosary is one and its parts are many, the rosary is not the same as its parts. When the parts are eliminated, there is no rosary which exists separately; therefore it is not inherently or fundamentally different from its parts. Because the rosary does not exist separate from its parts, it does not inherently depend on its parts, nor do the parts depend inherently on it. Also, the beads do not inherently belong to the rosary. Similarly, since the shape of the rosary is one of its qualities, this shape is not the rosary. Also, the collection of the beads and the string is the basis in dependence on which the rosary is imputed; therefore it is not the rosary."

In 1808, John Dalton propounded the atomic theory. He believed that an element actually consisted of separate indivisible and invisible atoms. He thought of atoms as things having the properties of a billiard ball. In the latter part of the century, scientists like Michael Faraday, James Maxwell and Lord Kelvin began their work in the field of electrical science. The electric nature of the atom was partly disclosed. In 1913, Neil Bohr of Copenhagen, propounded the theory according to which an atom consisted of two parts, a small heavy nucleus surrounded by a large empty region, in which electrons move somewhat like planets about the sun. Around the electrons, there are lines of magnetic force; the influence of these lines is theoretically universal. Faraday symbolized an atom as a starfish with a small body and comparatively long limbs which entangle the things the limbs contact. This might be put thus: the constituents of the material universe interact with one another and are really inseparable. This concept of the atom has important philosophical significance. Things do not exist individually. The existence of a single object is therefore nothing but a mental illusion. The universe is simply a process, a system of interconnected activities in which nothing moves independently of the rest and where all is in ceaseless motion. This is exactly the same principle, though different in words, as the Buddha's preaching of 'Annica', which means the impermanent or transient nature of things.

One of the most important edicts of Buddhism is a belief in a natural law called 'cause and effect', common to all worldly phenomena. This law is called 'Karma' in Sanskrit or 'Kamma' in Pali, the language of the Buddha. Karma is a force by virtue of which reaction follows action. According to Tibetan Buddhists, Buddha taught that one's present life is in a beginning-less series of rebirths and each of these is determined by one's actions in previous lives. This idea specifically refers to one's volitional actions, which may be good, bad or neutral. The Buddhist concept of karma is similar to Newton's Third Law of Motion, which holds that for every action there is a reaction. Similarly in Buddhism, actions give rise to concordant effects; good, bad and neutral experiences are the direct results of good, bad and neutral karma. This is presented as a universal law that has nothing to do with abstract ideas of justice, reward or punishments. Every action produces a concordant reaction, and this occurs automatically. It does not require the control, intervention or modification of any outside power, and as long as one remains within cyclic existence one performs actions (karma), and these evidently produce concordant results.

Buddhism teaches that one has transmigrated helplessly since the beginning-less time under the influence of ignorance and that ignorance has led to performance of actions that have created connections with cyclic existence. The world is full of suffering, aging and death, but most of us overlook these and focus on momentary pleasures. To those who view cyclic existence in accordance with reality, however, understand that all who are caught up in it must inevitably suffer over and over again. This truth was recognized with full existential clarity by the Buddha on the night of his enlightenment and he expressed it in a set of propositions, referred to by Buddhists as the Four Noble Truths. These are: 1. The truth of suffering 2. The truth of the origin of suffering 3. The truth of the cessation of suffering 4. The truth of the eightfold path, which overcomes suffering.

The truth of suffering holds that all of cyclic existence is inevitably connected with suffering. Dukkha or suffering refers not only to physical pain, but also to emotional turmoil, discomfort, dissatisfaction and sorrow. The truth of suffering is a recognition, that these things are found in the lives of ordinary beings and they generally view them as being unpleasant. Buddhism does not deny the presence of happiness in human life. What it does deny is that happiness can be permanent for those enmeshed in cyclic existence, which is characterized by constant change. Even when one finds happiness, it must inevitably end, only to be replaced by loss, longing and unhappiness. Buddha teaches a path by which this unsatisfactory situation may be ascended.

Buddhism is thus a psycho-ethical tradition, proceeding with a system of thought as well as definite path for realization and actualization. It is the system of only one problem and one solution with a path existing between the two. The only problem is the suffering of man, the solution is the attainment of the eternal state of bliss and the path between the two is the 'tri-stepped eightfold dharma'. Together the Four Noble Truths and the eightfold path constitute the way that leads to the attainment of Nirvana. Nirvana—the permanent, stable, imperishable, immovable, ageless, deathless, unborn and un-become, Nirvana—the power, bliss and happiness, the secure refuge, the shelter and the place of unassailable safety; Nirvana—the Real Truth and Supreme Reality; Nirvana—the supreme goal and the one and only consummation of our lives, the eternal, hidden and incomprehensible peace.

Almost every ancient religious teacher in every part of the world taught as the final goal of life an eternal mystical ethereal existence, far remote from the gross senses and the mass of suffering that these senses upbring. The concept of such eternal existence also catered well to the deeply inset longing of those who thirst for eternal existence the final abode into which the inner 'I' will escape and rest in peace for all eternity. The doctrine of Nirvana on the other hand taught the cessation of the 'I' wholly, with no remainder. The doctrine of Nirvana has meaning, and above has all practical import, purely from the doctrine of suffering. Were life not a suffering, Nirvana would not have been necessary.

Buddhism is often accused of being atheistic since Buddha makes no recognition of a personal God. This is the reason that led to the introduction of various forms of quasi-divine worship in Buddhism, because this creed was found too abstract and impersonal for popular acceptance. The Buddhist only looks up to the Buddha, the Awakened one, who saw the misery of the world, the dire conditions under which man lives, who is ill, poor and subject to adversity and death. He wanted to bring happiness to men, to help them to rid themselves of their hopelessness. This he did not by requiring them to plant their belief in a supernatural being, a God, or, even himself, though nearly perfect that he was. If a man is drowning, he does not enquire of those on the shore how deep the lake is, how cold the water is or to whom the lake belongs, his energies would only be consumed in overcoming the danger of drowning. Likewise, the belief in a deity, whether he created the lake, when he made the earth, whether or not the world is eternal, or whether it is finite or infinite. When a man wishes to disengage himself from a conceivably irretrievable position, metaphysical and theological speculations are of no avail. This is not to say that the Buddha condemned speculations regarding the age of the world, the nature of creation, etc. A scientist interested in geological formations leaves out of consideration what a physiologist has to say about the human body and its organs. When he needs such knowledge, he will apply to the physician, but not when he studies geological strata. Likewise Buddha construed that to a man in search of happiness and peace of mind, the curiosities regarding the creator and his creation, the universe, wouldn't help. He may be a philosopher, a theologian or a logician, or perhaps have solutions to metaphysical problems, but in his search for happiness, he has no need for such knowledge. A physician attending on the wounds of a man does not first ask him whether or not he goes to church. As a physician his job is to treat the person's wounds. In this sense Buddha was a physician of the soul and body and he proceeded scientifically by first diagnosing the malady. Buddhist thinking has always enjoyed the greatest freedom, untrammeled by dogmatism and authority of any kind, not even of the Buddha himself.

Buddha first experienced religion for himself. Nearly all religions demand a blind belief or faith because in its working out it deprives itself of the possibility of expounding truth. When incomprehensibilities form the foundations of thought, faith is demanded. Buddha warned men against adopting without analyzing. Because god is not something that man has found in his search, 'it' is something that man has conceptually assumed. Religion cannot be an acceptance of academic abstractions, assumptions or celebration of memories, but it should be a life of experience. Every individual must himself tread the path of realization, for only knowledge won out of experience has a life giving value. Buddhism is not an academic discipline, dealing only in words or symbols, seeking truth on a piece of paper. And the Buddha is not a deity. His teaching did not come to him from an extrasensory source. Remarkable though he was, he was a man, and learned and achieved all by the use of his sense receptors, limbs and brains. Buddhism is a science of experience.

Buddhism emerges before us now as a system which achieves an objective and detached view about the nature and destiny of man. This striking objectivity divorces the Buddhist system from the realm of religion. Buddhism is not properly a religion; it is a system for life and living in a world which is circumscribed with difficulty and beset with suffering. It is not a religion because it de-emphasizes faith in the unknown and unknowable and rejects dogmatism.

When Buddhism reached Tibet, about the seventh century AD, it had undergone a profound change. As taught by the Buddha in the 6th BC it was a special way of life laid down by the master for gentle ascetics and for men, later women who forsook their normal responsibilities for the homeless life of mendicants to end misery and suffering in the world and to attain salvation. It enjoined its followers to spread the word of the Buddha among the people they came in contact with. By their self-discipline and kindly demeanour, the followers of the Buddha were able to win the support of large classes of people. By the beginning of the Christian era, a vast literature began to develop, not just on the teachings of the Buddha and the rules of the order established by him but also on vast philosophical problems. These problems increased in complexity, as the Buddhists came into contact with other philosophical schools and had to restate their fundamental position in the accepted idiom. A large change came about in Buddhist philosophy and ethics when different Buddhist schools emerged and sought to reinterpret the teaching of the master. From the goal of individual salvation Buddhism moved to one seeking salvation of all sentient beings based on the unity of wisdom and universal compassion, the essence of Buddha's enlightenment.

With the assumption of the power by the Dalai Lama from 1642 onwards, an era of "harmonious blend of religion and politics", was established in Tibet. Buddhism has not been a mere system of beliefs to the Tibetans. It encompasses the entirety of their culture and civilization and constitutes the very essence of their lives. Buddhism permeated the daily lives of the Tibetan people and formed the social fabric connecting them to the land and the nature. As the influence of Buddhism grew, the impossible came to happen in Tibet. Previously they had organized and waged wars, raiding and conquering the territory in their neighbourhood, but due to the influence of Buddhism, the Tibetans underwent a change of heart and attitude, giving up their warring natures and creating a zone of peace in their country. The new international contexts in which Tibetan Buddhism must now survive, and indeed appears to thrive, coupled with weakening of traditional institutional regulation, have fostered an environment conducive to new and varied presentations of Buddhist teaching. Once largely a religion of Asian societies, Buddhism has demonstrated immense vitality in surviving massive socio-economic change, in contributing to the development of new ethnic and cultural identities in Asia, and in adapting to numerous modern contexts internationally, this adaptability to post-modern conditions is a result of a flexibility that stems from its internal diversity.

All over the world today there is growing interest in Buddhism. All those who are dissatisfied with traditional belief systems, who are disillusioned with the world as it is with all its ills and sufferings, and who seek rationally founded convincing answers to the questions of ultimate human concern, are turning to the study and practice of Buddhism. We do not have to prove the relevance of Buddhism in our contemporary situation, it is self-evident that Buddhism holds the future of mankind. In the real sense it is the only humanitarian and universal religion, which was propagated without fighting bloody wars. Buddhism as an active agent of world peace has begun to engage the serious attention not only of the politicians, statesmen, thinkers, sociologists and writers, but also of the common men and women looking for a way of life more satisfying than the present one. And so Buddhism and international living is bound to be a synonymous reality. Buddhism's universal appeal, socio-political viability, economic feasibility and its ethico-legal straight forwardness can lead the member states to world peace.

Verses from the Dhammapada

- Ere long, alas! This body will lie on the earth, despised, bereft of consciousness like a useless log (41).
- A misdirected mind will do us greater harm than what a hater may do to a hater or an enemy to an enemy (42).
- Neither a mother nor a father nor any other relative can do as much as a well directed mind can do for a man (43).
- The fool is tormented by such thoughts as 'these sons are mine', 'this wealth is mine' but he himself does not belong to himself. How then can sons and wealth belong to him (62).
- Fools of little understanding have themselves as their greatest enemies, for they perform evil deeds, which bear bitter fruits (66).
- The deed cannot be said to be well done, the performance of which brings repentance and the reward of which one receives weeping and with a tearful face (67).
- As a solid rock is not shaken by the wind, so wise people remain unmoved amidst praise and blame (81).
- Good people freely go on, no matter whatever happens to them; they do not prattle, craving for pleasure whether

touched by happiness or else by sorrow, wise people do not change in the manner of being elated or depressed (83).

- He is good wise and virtuous who does not wish for a son or for wealth or for lordship either for his own sake or the sake of others and who does not wish for his own success by unfair means (84).
- He whose appetites are appeased, who is indifferent to food, who has realized the emptiness of life and also realized the nature of unconditioned freedom, his path is difficult to understand, like that of birds flying in the air (93).
- Difficult it is to obtain birth as a human being; difficult is the hearing of the True Law; difficult is the birth of the awakened, that is, the attainment of Buddha-hood (182).
- To eschew all evil, to perform good actions and to purify one's mind – that is the teaching of the Buddhas (182).
- Passions cannot be satisfied even by means of a shower of gold pieces. He is wise who knows that passions have a short taste and cause pain (186).
- He who resorts to violence in any manner is not righteous, he who distinguishes between right and wrong, who is learned and leads others, not by violence but by law and equity and he who is guarded by the law and is intelligent, he is called righteous (256–57).
- A man is not learned because he talks much; he who is patient, free from hatred and fear, is said to be learned (258).

- A man who is envious, greedy and dishonest cannot become respectable merely by means of talking or on the account of the beauty of his complexion (262).
- Whatever is created is perishable, impermanent or transitory. He who realizes this, becomes indifferent to suffering. This is the way to purity (277).
- All created things are full of sorrow and sufferings; he who is wise enough to realize this becomes passive in suffering. This is the way that leads to purity (278).
- All the elements of the being are not self. When one is wise enough to realize this, one becomes indifferent to sorrow. This is the way to purity (279).

TWIN VERSES

1. If a man speaks or acts with an evil thought, pain follows him (as a consequence) as the wheel follows the foot of the ox, which draws the cart.
2. If a man speaks or acts with a pure thought, happiness follows him like a shadow that never leaves him.
3. 'He abused me, he beat me, he defeated me, he robbed me' – those who harbour such thoughts, will not be free from hatred.
5. Hatred never ceases through hatred; hatred ceases through love; this is the eternal law.
7. Some do not know that all of us must come to an end here; but those who know this, their disputes cease at once.

21. Earnestness is the path to immortality and thoughtlessness is the path to death. Those who are in earnest do not die; but those who are thoughtless are as if they are already dead.

50. One should take notice of one's own deeds of commission or omission but not of the unworthy actions of others nor their misdeeds of commission or omission.

51. The fine but fruitless words of him who does not act accordingly, are like a beautiful flower full of colour but lacking in scent.

58-59. Just as on a heap of rubbish thrown upon the highway, grows the lily, full of sweet fragrance and delightful even so among those who, like the rubbish, walk in darkness, the disciple of the truly enlightened Buddha, shines with glory by his wisdom.

103. If a man conquers thousand times thousand men in battles and if another conquers himself alone, he is the greatest of conquerors.

104-105. One's conquest of oneself is indeed better than one's conquest of others; not even god nor Gandhara nor Mara with Brahma could turn into defeat the victory of one who has conquered oneself.

125. If a man does wrong to a harmless, pure and innocent person, evil recoils on that fool even as fine dust thrown up against the wind recoils up against the person who threw it.

127. Not in the sky nor in the midst of the sea nor again the clefts of the mountains is there known a spot in

the whole world where a man might be freed from an evil deed or where death can be overcome.

129. All men tremble at punishment; all men fear death, remember you are like them so do not kill nor cause slaughter.

131. He who, in his search for happiness, punishes or kills beings, who also longs for happiness, will not find happiness after death.

136. A fool who commits evil deeds, does not know what will happen to him; but the wicked man burns through his own deeds, like one burnt by fire.

148. This body is worn out, full of diseases and frail. This heap of corruption breaks into pieces; life indeed ends in death.

150. After a citadel has been made of the bones, it is covered with flesh and blood and in it dwells old age and death, pride and deceit.

163. Bad deeds and deeds that are harmful to oneself, are easy to do; what is beneficial and good is very difficult to do.

167. Do not follow the evil law, do not live in thoughtlessness, do not follow false doctrines, do not be a friend of the world.

197. Let us live happily then, not hating those who hate us; let us live in freedom from hate, among men who hate us.

200. Let us live happily then, though there is nothing which we call our own. We shall be like the shining gods, feeding on happiness.

201. Victory breeds hatred; the conquered dwells in sorrow. He who has given up thoughts of both victory and defeat, he, the contented, is happy.

223. Let a man overcome anger by love; let him overcome evil by good, let him overcome the greedy by liberality and the liar by truth.

246-247. He who destroys truth, who speaks untruth, who in this world takes what is not given to him, who goes to another man's wife, who gives himself to drinking intoxicating liquors, he even in this world digs up his own root.

291. He who wishes to obtain pleasure by inflicting suffering on others, becomes entangled in the bonds of hatred, will never be free from hatred.

320. I shall endure abuses silently, just as the elephant in battle endures the arrow shot from the bow; for the majority of the people in the world are ill-natured.